Bread

FOR THE

Journey

Bread

FOR THE

Journey

MEDITATIONS
AND RECIPES
TO NOURISH
THE SOUL

Lovella Schellenberg, Anneliese Friesen, Betty Reimer,
Bev Klassen, Charlotte Penner, Ellen Bayles, Judy Wiebe,
Julie Klassen, Kathy McLellan, Marg Bartel

 **Herald Press**
Kitchener, Ontario
Harrisonburg, Virginia

Library and Archives Canada Cataloguing in Publication

Schellenberg, Lovella, 1959-, author
    Bread for the journey : meditations and recipes to nourish the soul
/ Lovella Schellenberg, Anneliese Friesen, Betty Reimer, Bev Klassen,
Charlotte Penner, Ellen Bayles, Judy Wiebe, Julie Klassen, Kathy
McLellan, Marg Bartel.

ISBN 978-1-5138-0048-6 (hardback)

    1. Devotional literature. 2. Mennonites--Prayers and devotions.
3. Cooking. 4. Cookbooks. I. Title.

BV4832.3.S34 2016   242'.2   C2016-901100-3

BREAD FOR THE JOURNEY
© 2016 by Herald Press, Kitchener, ON N2G 3R1
    Published simultaneously in the United States of America by Herald Press,
    Harrisonburg, VA 22802. All rights reserved.
Library of Congress Control Number: 2016932983
Canadian Entry Number: C2016-901100-3
International Standard Book Number: 978-1-5138-0048-6
Printed in Canada
Design by Reuben Graham
Cover photo by KucherAV / iStock / Thinkstock

Author photograph on p. 10 by Beatriz Photography. Other photographs by authors and from
authors' files.

For orders or information, call 800-245-7894 or visit HeraldPress.com.

20 19 18 17 16   10 9 8 7 6 5 4 3 2 1

We dedicate this book and our royalties
to orphans and widows who face each day in need.

Our prayer is that they would see the love of Jesus
extended through caring hands,
one home and one heart at a time.

All author royalties from *Bread for the Journey*, as well as from the Mennonite
Girls Can Cook cookbooks, go to nourish children around the world.

CONTENTS

Mennonite Girls Can Cook authors, from left: Charlotte Penner, Anneliese Friesen, Julie Klassen, Judy Wiebe, Bev Klassen (kneeling), Kathy McLellan, Betty Reimer, Ellen Bayles, Lovella Schellenberg, and Marg Bartel (kneeling).

INTRODUCTION

A reader of our recipe blog, *Mennonite Girls Can Cook*, once asked why so many of our Sunday posts are called Bread for the Journey when no bread recipes are included in them. We explained that these posts address a spiritual hunger. Early on in our daily posting of recipes, we decided to set aside the Lord's Day as a day of rest from our kitchens so that we might not forget the bread that nourishes our souls.

Bread is the food of hope. The ten of us share a common heritage, which includes stories of persecution, hunger, and migration. We tell some of those stories in this book. Persecuted for their stand on baptism and pacifism, our German Anabaptist forebears ended up in Russia (Ukraine), where they found themselves in difficult times once again when faced by war and communism. Yet, even when they lost everything, as long as they had bread, there was hope.

Bread made our grandmothers feel prepared for whatever lay ahead. They would bake *Zwieback*, a type of roll, and slowly roast them to a dry husk so that they could be kept for months. These became a staple to send along when a family member left home or when visiting someone sick or in prison. Marlene Epp writes in *Sisters or Strangers?* that "the roasting of and packing in sacks of zwieback became a ritual of hope and moving forward."

Bread is also comfort food. Sacks of toasted *Zwieback* sustained our grandparents and parents as refugees on their journey across the ocean. *Zwieback* brought them through hard times of resettlement. Fresh *Zwieback* also became a staple in celebratory settings such as gatherings and weddings. Most of us authors have memories of our mothers baking *Zwieback* on Saturdays in preparation for Sunday *Faspa*, a simple meal served to anyone who might drop by for a visit.

Before the feeding of the five thousand, Jesus looked at the great crowd and wondered aloud where they could buy enough bread to feed the people. The disciples simply could not collect enough bread to feed so many. But Jesus found a way. Of course he would! He was showing people that by meeting their physical need, he could meet their spiritual need as well.

The day after Jesus fed the five thousand, some of the people who had been fed were looking for him. He told them, "Do not work for food that spoils, but for food that endures to eternal life, which the Son of Man will give you" (John 6:27 NIV). Jesus also told them, "I am the bread of life. Whoever comes to me will never go hungry. . . . Whoever eats this bread will live forever" (John 6:35, 51 NIV). These words have caused some listeners, both then and now, to be offended. But to those who have believed, they have become words of life.

This is our prayer: that as you read these portions of spiritual truth, you will feel more prepared for whatever tasks await you. We pray that these devotionals, recipes, and family stories will nourish you for your own journey ahead.

As you read, may you find comfort and hope in Jesus, who is the bread of life.

Lovella   *Anneliese*

Recipe
ZWIEBACK

Yields 48 medium or 60 small buns

- 2 cups / 500 ml milk
- ¾ cup / 175 ml butter, cubed
- 1 cup / 250 ml very cold water
- 2 tablespoons / 30 ml sugar

- 2 tablespoons / 30 ml instant or fine-grain quick-rising yeast
- 1 tablespoon / 15 ml salt
- 6½–7 cups / 1.5–1.75 L flour, divided

1. Heat milk in a saucepan. Add butter and allow to melt. Remove from heat.
2. Add cold water. Combined butter, milk, and water should be warm but not hot.
3. In large mixing bowl (a stand mixer with hook attachment is helpful), mix sugar, yeast, and salt. Add warm liquids and stir in 2 cups / 500 ml flour. Let sit for about 5–10 minutes until frothy.

4. Continue adding flour, ½ cup / 125 ml at a time. Knead until dough is easy to shape into a soft ball by hand, using a light dusting of flour if too sticky.

5. Place dough in a bowl large enough for dough to double or triple in size.

6. Cover with a clean tea towel. Cover towel with plastic wrap to keep warmth in. Let rise about 1–1½ hours, until dough has spread and risen to at least double.

7. Grease three baking sheets with shortening or butter.

8. With greased hands, gently loosen dough along sides of bowl to deflate.

9. Grease hands and pinch off from the edge a piece of dough about the size of an orange. Shape it by holding it with both hands and folding sides under until top is smooth.

10. Holding dough in your left hand as if you're holding a cup of coffee, squeeze a bit of dough, about the size of a walnut, between your thumb and forefinger. You may help push it up with your right hand. Pinch your thumb and forefinger together to squeeze it off. With your right hand, take the bun and place it on the pan. Reposition or reshape dough so that the top is smooth again. Squeeze the dough between your thumb and forefinger again, this time pinching off a smaller bun, about half the size of the first. Squeeze it off and place it on top of the first bun, making sure that the pinched-off end faces down. Repeat the same method to make remaining rolls.

11. With an index finger, poke the top of each bun so that there is an indentation in the roll.

12. Place about 20 small buns per large baking sheet. Do not crowd the buns; leave room for a second rise. Cover buns loosely with a tea towel and plastic wrap. Let rise 45–60 minutes.

13. Bake at 400° F / 205° C for 18–20 minutes until golden brown. Remove to cooling racks.

What can I say about this most traditional Mennonite bun, which generations have grown up with and now is a favorite treat for my grandchildren? I realize that I have become somewhat like the moms and grandmothers before me: I do not need to follow the exact recipe, and they always turn out. Forming the rolls takes a bit of practice, but it does get easier over time. In times past, potato water was saved and added as liquid to the buns. The water-to-milk ratio can be very loose, and an egg can be added. My mom made *Zwieback* on Saturdays so that she could serve them fresh with Sunday dinner's soup or *Faspa* in the afternoon. We don't butter them, as they already have a nice buttery flavor, but we do love them with jam and Havarti cheese.

Reistche Tweiback (or *Geröstete Zwieback* as we called them in High German) are less common today, but they were a staple when there was no way to keep the buns fresh. Once the *Zwieback* buns were a couple of days old, they were roasted on low heat for about 1–1½ hours. Dipped in tea, coffee, or sugar, these dry husks are a treat and a comfort food.

Anneliese

WEEK 1

Family Journeys
ADOPTING ARON

I wonder if my Grandma Klassen, who was expecting her thirteenth child during a time of revolution, worried about what would happen to the baby she was carrying. She died while he was yet an infant, and so her family had no other option but to trust God's love for the little one.

Her baby, Aron, was to become my father. He was born in the Mennonite village of Suworovka, Orenburg, Russia, in 1918, a year after the Bolsheviks overthrew the czar's government. The village struggled to survive, and by 1920 the few seeds that they managed to hide from marauding robbers failed to grow because the rain they desperately needed did not come.

Above: Katherina and Bernhard Peters and their adopted son, Aron, Lovella's father.

In the same village, a young couple, Bernhard and Katherina Peters, who did not have any children, asked my grandpa if he would consider allowing Aron to become their own. Grandpa Klassen, who would later starve to death, agreed that Aron should go live with the Peters. After Aron and another adopted child named Eleanor joined the family, Bernhard and Katherina courageously decided to immigrate to Canada.

Packing enough clothes for travel, a few photos, and a blueprint of the estate they walked away from, they said a tearful goodbye, knowing they might never see loved ones again. In Moscow they were delayed when the children became seriously ill with measles. Eventually they were able to travel to England, where they boarded a vessel and arrived in Saint John, New Brunswick, on March 22, 1925. Though they arrived with very little in terms of earthly possessions, they were thankful to be free from communism and to be able once again to worship without fear of reprisals.

They said a tearful goodbye,
knowing they might never see loved ones again.

In Waldheim, Saskatchewan, they were given shelter, where they slept four crosswise on one bed. Understanding no English, Aron and Eleanor were sent to school. If the language barrier and the visible poverty were not daunting enough, they also soon realized that their clothing at once marked them as "Russländer."

Years later, on a flight to Germany, Aron mentioned that he was going to be reunited with his family. The pilot heard about this special trip and invited my dad to see the sunrise from the cockpit. Upon seeing the brilliant red sky, my father marveled that after seventy years he would be reunited with his two remaining biological siblings. He declared, "God's great love has made this possible."

Upon meeting, the three of them embraced: my dad; his elderly sister, dressed in her Sunday best; and his older brother, who expressed a long-awaited greeting, "*Mein liebster Bruder*" (My dearest brother).

In his seventies, Dad wrote his life story for our family. Realizing that putting on paper what he had experienced in life would not come naturally, he began by writing, "May God give me grace to write how He led me in my life that it may not be an offence but a blessing to others."

My dad's life was a blessing to so many.

Lorella

Recipe

LOADED BAKED POTATO SOUP

Serves 4

- 1 (12-ounce / 350-g) package bacon, diced
- 4 large russet potatoes, peeled and cubed
- 3 cups / 750 ml chicken stock
- ¼ cup / 60 ml butter
- 1 large onion, chopped
- ¼ cup / 60 ml flour
- 2 cups / 500 ml milk
- 1 cup / 100 g cheddar cheese, shredded
- ½ teaspoon / 2 ml salt
- ¼ teaspoon / 1 ml pepper
- 3 green onions, sliced
- Sour cream as garnish (optional)

1. Cook bacon until crisp. Drain on paper towel.
2. Place potatoes and chicken stock in large pot and bring to a boil. Reduce heat and simmer for about 15 minutes, or until potatoes are tender. With slotted spoon, remove several scoops of potatoes. Place in a bowl, mash, and set aside.
3. In a small saucepan, melt butter. Add the chopped onion and sauté until tender. Stir in flour and cook for about 1 minute. Whisk in milk, a little at a time, bringing to a boil and simmering until thickened. Add cheese, salt, and pepper, and stir until cheese is melted.
4. Slowly stir cheese sauce into soup pot with the potatoes and chicken stock. Bring to a boil on low heat.
5. Add mashed potatoes, three-quarters of the crispy bacon, and half the sliced green onions. Stir to combine. Heat through.
6. To serve, ladle into individual soup bowls and top with additional shredded cheese, bacon, green onions, and a dollop of sour cream.

Why not combine your favorite baked potato flavors in a soup and serve it up in a bowl? Just the thought of enjoying a bowl of loaded baked potato soup is enough to take the chill off a cool day!

Judy

Week 1, Day 1
"THANKFULS"

Rejoice always, pray continually, give thanks in all circumstances; for this is God's will for you in Christ Jesus. —1 THESSALONIANS 5:16-18 (NIV)

A few years ago I opened a gift that had come in the mail. It was a little blue journal that my daughter-in-law suggested I use as a gratitude journal. I now keep it in plain view in our family room, and each day I try to write down two or three "thankfuls."

Here are just a few of them: A walk in the park. God's protection. A visit around a fire pit. Sleeping in. Rhubarb pie. God's Word to encourage. *Rollkuchen* and watermelon. Forgiveness. A day at home in the kitchen. The dads raising our grands. Lunch with my girls. Watching cousins play. Coffee brewing. A husband who loves coming home. Peach jam. Health. The pitter-patter of rain. A good book to read. Talking to God anytime. Holding a newborn. My heritage. Seeing traditions passed on in my kids. The smell of wet earth. Clean windows.

When we give thanks to God, we acknowledge that every gift is from him. The Bible says that God causes his sun to rise on the evil and the good and that he sends rain on the righteous and the unrighteous (Matthew 5:45).

Yet I can't help but wonder: Is God a little like us, in that we find it so much more fun to give to someone who appreciates a gift? Does God smile when we say thank you for the little gifts of each day?

Anneliese

PRAY
God, you have given me so many gifts. Open my eyes to see those gifts today.

SAVOR
What are a few of your "thankfuls" for today?

Week 1, Day 2
UNITY AS SISTERS

Offer hospitality to one another without grumbling. Each of you
should use whatever gift you have received to serve others, as faithful
stewards of God's grace in its various forms. —1 PETER 4:9-10 (NIV)

In 2010, the ten of us "Mennonite girls" met together for our first
summit. It was the first time we all met in person and gathered
around the table together.

Our story had begun a few years earlier, when Lovella put out an
invitation to submit recipes to her personal blog. At first it was just a
fun way to share our favorite Mennonite and other family recipes. Little did we know that God would soon turn our love for cooking and
baking into a ministry. It was around that table in August 2010 that
we celebrated God's leading and the gift of friendship.

We share a love of cooking and hospitality, but more importantly,
we all love Jesus. It's our faith in God that has given us unity and purpose as we use the gifts God has uniquely given to each one of us.

It's a joy to serve the Lord together, and to be able to share our
faith individually and as a group of women through the ministry God

has given us. We count it a privilege to give the royalties of our books to the cause of Christ around the world. There's nothing like the feeling of fellowship with sisters in the Lord.

It's a lovely thing to share recipes and stories from our kitchens. But lovelier still is the feeling of unity that we have as sisters in the Lord.

Kathy

PRAY

Thank you, God, for the gift of Christian sisters. Help me to call on my sisters in times of need.

SAVOR

How can you nurture friendships with sisters in Christ?

Week 1, Day 3
STONES OF REMEMBRANCE

Then Samuel took a stone and set it up between Mizpah and Shen and called its name Ebenezer; for he said, "Till now the Lord has helped us." —1 SAMUEL 7:12 (ESV)

The milestones of life are meant to be marked and celebrated. We gather friends and family together and cement a particular moment with an event or a celebration that becomes a "stone of remembrance." We celebrate the birth of each child in our family and then mark every year by throwing a party. Each step along the way is a milestone to be marked: baptism, graduation, engagement, marriage, and anniversaries. And when the journey comes to an end, despite our tears, we can celebrate the lives of our dear ones. Life is meant to be celebrated, and in doing that, we are honoring the Giver of life.

We have celebrated several milestone occasions in our family recently. My husband and I had our fortieth wedding anniversary not long ago, and we marked that milestone by taking our family on a vacation. I turned sixty. That called for many celebrations, big and small. My father had his ninetieth birthday recently. The family came together, and we celebrated this man who is our dad, granddad, and great-grandad.

Each milestone is a reason to celebrate! Though our journey in life is mostly about pressing forward, milestone occasions are the perfect time to stop and reflect. As Samuel did so long ago, we can erect a marker on that spot and acknowledge that it is God who has helped us to reach it. And we can go forward, knowing that God will complete what he has begun in us. The apostle Paul wrote, "And I am sure of this, that he who began a good work in you will bring it to completion at the day of Jesus Christ" (Philippians 1:6 ESV). He who has been faithful to every milestone marker along the way will be faithful to the end.

Judy

PRAY

God, thank you for your faithfulness throughout my life. As I reflect on your goodness and great love that brought me to each milestone in my life, I give you the praise!

SAVOR

What "stones of remembrance" have you placed recently? How has God been faithful to you in times of celebration and transition?

Week 1, Day 4
ENTERTAINING ANGELS

Do not forget to show hospitality to strangers, for by so doing some people have shown hospitality to angels without knowing it. —HEBREWS 13:2 (NIV)

Hospitality is taught by example in most Mennonite homes. Friends, family, and neighbors know they are welcome at any time. In my childhood home and many others, it was not unusual to invite strangers for a meal—the farmhands, new neighbors, a family in need.

The Bible urges each person to show hospitality to those around them and to do it generously and without complaining (1 Peter 4:9). Hospitality is also listed as one of the spiritual gifts especially given to some individuals (Romans 12:6-8).

So many people think that hospitality requires a special, attractive table and a fancy meal. However, in our busy lives, most of us don't have the time or inclination to do this. The hospitality the Bible speaks of merely requires that we willingly share what we have with others. Today that might be a bowl of soup, take-out pizza, a cup of coffee, or a beautifully prepared meal. It might be a warm bed, the offer of a ride, or a place to stay when misfortune strikes. All are ways to show hospitality to one another.

Don't forget to extend that same hospitality to your children, your parents, and yes, even yourself. In doing so, you are a living example of the grace God has extended to you. As Hebrews 13:2 says, you might even find yourself showing "hospitality to angels without knowing it"!

Week 1, Day 5
BEANS AND RICE

Then the righteous will answer him, saying, "Lord, when did we see you hungry and feed you, or thirsty and give you drink? And when did we see you a stranger and welcome you, or naked and clothe you? And when did we see you sick or in prison and visit you?" And the King will answer them, "Truly, I say to you, as you did it to one of the least of these my brothers, you did it to me." —MATTHEW 25:37-40 (ESV)

When I look through my cookbooks for ideas on what to make for supper, the choices are endless. How privileged we are to have food to eat. Not only do we have food; we have a multitude of choices about what kind of food to buy and prepare.

Sometimes I prepare a simple meal of beans and rice. This dish is to remind us of how most of the world eats. There are millions of people who have nothing to eat; for them, beans and rice would be a real treat.

Jesus calls us to feed the hungry, help the poor, visit the sick, and welcome the lonely. Sometimes we give money to causes that help the poor, and that's a good thing. But do we ask ourselves, who are the lonely and the poor in my circle? Who is sick that I could visit and encourage this week?

"True evangelical faith . . . cannot lay dormant," wrote Menno Simons, after whom the Mennonites are named. "It clothes the naked; feeds the hungry; consoles the afflicted; shelters the miserable; aids and consoles all the oppressed; [and] binds up that which is wounded."

What is my responsibility as a follower of Jesus? What can I do? I may not be able to feed all the hungry in the world, but I can create an awareness among my family and friends. I can tell them about why I am serving beans and rice today. I can be thankful for all that has been given to me, and I can do my small part in building God's kingdom.

PRAY

Lord, turn my thoughts to gratitude today. Help me to serve you through serving the least of these.

SAVOR

What action can you take today on behalf of the "least of these"?

Week 1, Day 6

GOD'S HANDIWORK

---

*The heavens declare the glory of God, and the sky
above proclaims his handiwork.* —PSALM 19:1 (ESV)

It has been a privilege to raise our family in beautiful British Columbia. We are blessed with diverse and amazing places to enjoy, and
we experience God's creation right in our own backyard. Ever since
my children were young, we have celebrated outdoor adventures
together as a family. I remember taking them for walks around the
glistening emerald lakes. I remember buckling up their boots and
untangling their skis. I remember sitting around evening campfires
and strumming a guitar while their tired heads nodded off to sleep.
These times have brought us together to stand in awe of God's beauty
around us.

In winter, when the clouds part, we can see endless snowcapped
mountains towering above us. There is nothing more exhilarating
than making fresh powdery tracks down the mountainside with our
skis, inhaling and exhaling breaths of crisp air, feeling the fresh chilly
breezes on our faces, and listening to nature speak its own language.

During the summer months, these mountains are transformed into moss-carpeted rain forests, which allow for endless hours of hiking, cycling, fishing, and camping. We can watch a vibrant sun setting over a rich, rugged landscape dotted with pristine lakes and rivers.

The song "Creation Calls" by Brian Doerksen invites us to take in stunning glimpses of God's masterpiece, glimpses that then allow us to glorify, worship, and draw our minds to new places of intimacy with him. The last words of the song—"I believe just like a child"— invite us to come back to a childlike state of awe. Returning to the lakesides and mountains year after year, generation after generation—these things help us enjoy the simple pleasures of this earth with our children and grandchildren, build lifelong memories, and share God's truth.

There is nothing like the feeling of standing in the great outdoors and listening to the voice of God. Such moments of intimacy reinforce my relationship with God the Creator.

Marg

PRAY

Thank you, Creator God, for your marvelous creation. I am in awe of the beauty of your world.

SAVOR

Where have you felt most in awe of God's creation?

MOST AMAZING GIFT

But when the goodness and loving kindness of God our Savior appeared, he saved us, not because of works done by us in righteousness, but according to his own mercy, by the washing of regeneration and renewal of the Holy Spirit. —TITUS 3:4-5 (ESV)

Don't you just love giving gifts to deserving people? I usually have a few little things, such as chocolates and gift cards for coffee shops, tucked away in drawers. I always look forward to pulling them out and giving them to people. Sometimes, we have been led to help financially when we have been made aware of a need.

Sure—it's easy to give lovely gifts to people who are nice to us. It can be harder to give a gift to someone we feel has slighted or wronged us. Yet God showers us with the gift of compassion whether we are deserving or not.

When God asked Jonah to go tell the people of Nineveh to repent, Jonah ran in the opposite direction. After he realized that he could not disobey God, Jonah decided to go. But then he was unhappy because he expected that the people of Nineveh might repent, and he thought that they did not deserve God's compassion. So Jonah went into the city, told the Ninevites to repent, and, as we know, they did. The people in the city seriously demonstrated that they would turn from their evil ways. God had compassion on the residents of the city who had sinned in every conceivable way. They were not destroyed but rather saved.

The Bible is clear that sin is sin. I sometimes find it hard to fathom that I need to repent just as much as the most evil person in the world. God, who sees my heart, sees me for who I am. In his vast love, he chose to give me—and all of us—the most amazing gift we could ever imagine. God sent his Son, Jesus, to die on the cross for us. In his mercy, he forgave our sins and gave us new life in Jesus Christ.

Humanly, it makes no sense. No wonder we call God's compassion for us "amazing grace."

God's love is the same for all of us. We only need to see our sins, repent, and then accept and believe in Jesus. I am so thankful for the gift I did not deserve but that was given in grace.

Lorella

PRAY

God, thank you for the most amazing gift: Jesus. Thank you for new life in Christ.

SAVOR

What sins do you need to repent of today? Ask God to forgive you, and receive his amazing grace.

WEEK 2

Family Journeys
AN ANGEL IN THE PARLOR

I will never forget the story that *Oma* (Grandma) shared with me
when I was about sixteen years old. I remember sitting at the
kitchen table in my father's parents' house when Oma told me the tale.
In many ways, it's a story that changed my life.

My paternal grandmother had just birthed her first child, my uncle
Jacob. He was about six weeks old when she and her young husband
decided to travel to her parents' village to introduce their new son to
the family. She was excited to share this joyful time with her family.
Little did she know that it would be a fatal trip and would change her
life forever.

*Above: Charlotte's grandmother Maria Klassen is seated at left in this photograph, which was taken in
about 1915, prior to her wedding and the massacre.*

It was the end of October 1919. That night Makhnov bandits came to her parents' village on horseback and pillaged, raped inhabitants, and brutally attacked the village, called Eichenfeld at the time. The bandits forcefully entered the homestead, attacked Oma's mother and sister, and killed her husband, father, and brother. Oma was terrified, and tried to hide somewhere in the house with her infant son. Shortly after she entered the parlor, looking for some place to hide, a bandit came in and ransacked the room, looking for something of value. She stood completely still, praying he would not notice her. Not once did he make eye contact with her or acknowledge her presence. Oma told me she felt as though an angel of the Lord stood in front of her, with wings spread out to shield her and protect her and the baby.

> *She felt as though an angel of the Lord*
> *stood in front of her, with wings spread out*
> *to shield her and protect her and the baby.*

Once the bandits left, Oma frantically searched for her beaten mother and sister, hardly believing the horror that she had just witnessed. The women, children, and any other survivors walked to the neighboring village in search of refuge.

My mother's father was also from that same village. Only he and his youngest brother survived that night. *Opa* (Grandpa) and his brother were seven and five years old and left orphaned in desperate times.

Never did I ever imagine that some thirty years after hearing that story, I would have the privilege to go back to that very village. My aunt Tina invited me to go with her and a tour group of people from Canada and the United States on a trip back to the scene of horror. There we got to lay a marker on the mass grave in which the families of my paternal Oma and maternal Opa were buried, and we were able to honor the ones who lost their lives that night.

My aunt Tina was asked to unveil the monument, and I was privileged to read all the names of the ones believed to be buried there. What an emotional day to finally honor them with a Christian funeral ceremony. It was hard to believe such violence could occur in such a picturesque and serene place. I wondered at the horrors my family experienced and the strong faith in Jesus to which they clung.

When I asked my family members who had gone through so much trauma how they made it through all the horror, this was their answer to me: "You have two choices. One is to embitter yourself to God, and the other is to trust God." They chose to trust and to cling to him.

Having this opportunity to go back to my family's village made me feel as though I had come full circle. They did not leave me earthly riches. Instead, they gave me the greatest treasure of all: a strong heritage of faith and trust in God.

Recipe

BEAVER TAILS

Yields 12 "tails"

- ¾ cup / 175 ml warm milk
- 3 tablespoons / 45 ml oil
- 1 egg
- 2 tablespoons / 30 ml sugar

- ¾ teaspoon / 3 ml salt
- 1 tablespoon / 15 ml instant yeast
- 3⅓ cups / 825 ml flour
- Canola oil (for frying)

1. In a large mixing bowl, stir together milk, oil, egg, sugar, and salt.
2. Stir in 2 cups / 500 ml flour and the yeast. Knead 4 minutes, adding the rest of the flour as needed to make a smooth and elastic dough.
3. Place in a greased bowl, cover, and let rise in a warm place for 45 minutes.
4. Gently knead dough to deflate. Pinch off about 12 golf ball–sized pieces of dough.

5. Place one dough ball on a greased surface, press down, and stretch it with your fingers into a fairly flat oval shape, similar to a beaver's tail. Repeat with other pieces.
6. Heat 4 inches / 10 cm canola oil in a pot or fryer. The temperature of the oil should reach 385° F / 195° C.
7. Gently lower the flattened dough pieces into oil, approximately two at a time so that your cooking temperature remains the same. (Frying more at a time can lower the heat of the oil.)
8. Fry both sides of the dough until golden brown.
9. Remove fried dough from the oil and place on paper towel to absorb the excess oil.

Topping
- ¼ cup / 60 ml sugar
- 1 teaspoon / 5 ml cinnamon

1. Mix sugar and cinnamon together in a bowl.
2. Toss the fried beaver tails in this mixture until fully coated on both sides. (We usually leave a few uncoated so they can be enjoyed with syrup or a favorite jam.)

When I was growing up, these beaver tails were a special treat on bread-baking day. Coming home from school, we were always hungry, and this treat smelled so good. Mom would always set aside a portion of dough from bread-baking and would just be finished frying it up as we walked in the door. We would gather around the kitchen table and spread syrup or jam on these warm pieces of fried bread dough. My mom never made too many; we would eat every last one! She used to call them *lada koki*, which means "cookies like leather" in Low German. Later on I made them for our children and then our grandchildren.

OUR STORY TO TELL

"Love the Lord your God with all your heart and with all your soul and with all your strength. These commandments that I give you today are to be on your hearts. Impress them on your children. Talk about them when you sit at home and when you walk along the road, when you lie down and when you get up. . . . Be careful that you do not forget the Lord, who brought you out of Egypt, out of the land of slavery." —DEUTERONOMY 6:5-7, 12 (NIV)

Some of my earliest and most vivid memories of learning about God are of my paternal grandmother telling me about her hardships in Russia and the heavenly home she was waiting for. While she strummed her guitar, teaching me the lyrics to *"Gott ist die Liebe,"* or as I sat on her bed, combing her long, greying hair, which she would then twist into a tiny bun, she described heaven as if she had been there.

The stories my grandparents and parents shared with me over the years ingrained in me an awareness of God's protection and leading, beginning with our Anabaptist forebears fleeing Europe to live in Russia and eventually moving to a country where we can enjoy peace and prosperity. Despite hunger, imprisonment, war, family separation, and the loss of loved ones, our grandparents continued to trust in God even when communism banned all manner of religious practice. Their faith, and God's provision through it all, is a story to share, sometimes even through a simple thing such as preparing our "strange" ethnic foods. If *Borscht* and *Zwieback* give me an excuse to tell my grandchildren of our past, then they are good things. As grandparents, especially, we have a legacy of time and experience to draw on for wisdom and patience as we remember God's patience with us.

No matter our background, we all have a story to tell. Not all of us have ancestors who worshiped God, but all of us have the chance to begin a new story of hope by accepting God's invitation to become part of his family. By learning to love and forgive, lending a listening ear, and letting our families know that we are praying for them, we can pass on the greatest gift we have: a personal relationship with a loving God, expressed in daily life.

Anneliese

PRAY	SAVOR
God, thank you for the legacy of faith that others have passed on to me. Help me to tell my story to younger generations.	*Who told you stories of their relationship with God? How did their stories form you?*

Week 2, Day 2

WHAT KIND OF PILLARS?

Therefore we do not lose heart. Though outwardly we are wasting away, yet inwardly we are being renewed day by day. —2 CORINTHIANS 4:16 (NIV)

A few summers ago we took a drive down to Bryce Canyon, a national park nestled in southwestern Utah. I am awed by the beauty of this park, how the process of erosion forms pinnacles and pillars into an array of fantastic shapes. One can see how tiny drops of water have built beautiful monuments and pinnacles.

I can identify with John Muir, who said that nature is a great teacher. "In every walk of nature, one receives far more than he seeks," Muir wrote. For me there is no greater joy than to be out in nature and feel God. Nature reveals the mind of God.

Each one of us also goes through an erosion process. Just as a single thought finds its way into our mind, it leaves sediment that sinks deep down into our soul, forming pillars of character.

Sometimes we may be buffeted by stress and pressed by challenges that come at us from the outside. We may collapse under external pressure. At other times we might let immoral and selfish thoughts fill our minds. They become eroding pillars of evil.

But when we fill our minds with truth and love, we form strong and beautiful pillars in our souls. When we pursue God, we reflect his character in our lives.

Just as Bryce Canyon was developed over thousands of years, so our true characters are also being shaped and formed into Christlikeness. This process shows the real resurrection power of Christ, who strengthens us moment by moment.

Marg

PRAY	SAVOR
God, shape me and mold me in your image. Form my character after your Son's.	*What kind of pillars are you erecting in your life?*

Week 2, Day 3
BEAVER TEETH

But seek first the kingdom of God and his righteousness, and all these things will be added to you. —MATTHEW 6:33 (ESV)

At the park where I walk, there is evidence of a busy creature at work. A beaver has clearly been doing his job. It amazes me how, literally overnight, numerous beautiful trees are felled along the creek, falling into the water and never on the path. To us who enjoy the beauty of the park, it can be rather disturbing. Some concerned soul recently surrounded several very large trees with wiring to protect them. In the beaver's defense, he is only doing his job.

Did you know that a beaver's teeth never stop growing? Chewing wood actually helps to keep a beaver's teeth from getting too long. The beaver's teeth are made to chew wood.

To build a shelter, the beaver must use his God-given tools and keep at the job. Of course, that beaver could look at a tall tree and figure that it's way too big of a project to take on. But in using what he has been given—those amazing teeth—and sticking to the task, he finds success.

What are my priorities today? What shelter must I build? What steps will help me achieve it? And what has God given me so that I can focus and get the task done?

Sometimes the trees in our lives seem so large. Thank God that he has given us the teeth and the tenacity to face them.

Anneliese

PRAY

God, thank you for giving me what I need to serve you. Help me to identify the talents and tools you've given me to do my work for your kingdom.

SAVOR

What large obstacles might you face today? What are the "beaver teeth"—tools and talents—that you can use to overcome them?

Week 2, Day 4

OBEYING GOD

"If you obey the commandments of the Lord your God that I command you today, by loving the Lord your God, by walking in his ways, and by keeping his commandments and his statutes and his rules, then you shall live and multiply, and the Lord your God will bless you in the land that you are entering to take possession of it." —DEUTERONOMY 30:16 (ESV)

When my grandnephew was two years old, he was scolded for being disobedient at the dinner table. When told he needed to obey and eat his food properly, he announced to his mother, "But I don't want to obey!"

I love his honesty. Sometimes I don't want to obey either, but I'd never say it outright! I am more passive aggressive in my disobedience than he is.

When God reveals an area of my life that needs a change, I really test him. "Is that really what you want me to do?" I say with some hemming and hawing. "Is that really your voice? Like, right now? How about next week? Can we go slowly in that direction?" Sometimes I can ignore God completely.

There are times when obedience does come more easily to me. What sweet times those are! I want to be a more trusting child of God. I want to be able to say yes more quickly to whatever God wants from me. I want to be in God's Word more so that I know what he requires of me in this relationship with him.

I'm remembering the song we used to sing in Sunday school: "Trust and obey / for there's no other way / to be happy in Jesus / than to trust and obey."

Simple but true. Let's be honest: like my grandnephew, sometimes we just don't want to obey. But if we obey God's commands, we can be assured that God will bless us, and that we will receive deep joy when we walk in his ways.

Elle

PRAY

God, help me to trust and obey you. Give me a heart of obedience to your Word and your way.

SAVOR

Are you honest with God when you don't want to obey him? Tell God about the times that you don't want to obey his commands, and ask him to give you that desire.

Week 2, Day 5
CHEERLEADERS

But encourage one another daily, as long as it is called "Today," so that none of you may be hardened by sin's deceitfulness. —HEBREWS 3:13 (NIV)

I have so enjoyed watching my grandchildren run races and partici-pate in sporting events these past few years. Some time ago my twin granddaughters were in a long-distance run that came by our house. As the runners passed our place, I went out to cheer and noticed that our son was running alongside his girls.

What an encouragement for them to have someone spurring them on, giving them words of hope and cheer. The race became easier for them, and they just knew they could do it.

We are called to be encouragers, to give hope to others along the journey of life. We have a wonderful example of one who did that well in the New Testament: the apostle Paul. He knew that the early Christians needed to be urged on to "fight the good fight of faith" (1 Timothy 6:12 NIV).

Things haven't changed a whole lot since those days. Believers still need to hear words of encouragement. How good are you at handing them out to others? We get so wrapped up in our daily living that we tend to forget about others who may be in need of a little message of hope.

Do those in your household and those closest to you hear words of encouragement from you? What about your friends? Do you spur them on, cheer them up, and make them smile?

Those around us need to know that we care about them. They will be capable of great things just knowing they have cheerleaders!

Judy

PRAY

Dear heavenly Father, teach me to be an encourager. Help me to give hope to those who have lost sight of the finish line, and to run alongside of those who feel they can't go on.

SAVOR

Who can you be a cheerleader for this week?

Week 2, Day 6
FAITH INTO ACTION

But if anyone has the world's goods and sees his brother in need, yet closes his heart against him, how does God's love abide in him? Little children, let us not love in word or talk but in deed and in truth. —1 JOHN 3:17-18 (ESV)

I was privileged to be part of a team of women from our church who went to Haiti on an exposure tour with Compassion Canada. What an example of resilience and faith the Haitian people were to us! Although they live with physical poverty, they have a wealth we do not possess, in grateful hearts, generous spirits, and strong faith.

Our Haitian guide told us that when the Haiti earthquake happened, many people turned their lives over to God. Church attendance has increased, and among those we worshiped with on the fourth anniversary of the earthquake, we saw nothing but thankfulness and praise. Instead of defeat and despair, we saw people doing what they could to address the physical and spiritual poverty around them.

We were blessed to be part of a women's conference. Despite the differences in our economic circumstances, we have so much in common. We accompanied several of them into their homes and were able to help with the things all moms around the world do: doing laundry, cooking meals, bathing children. We share the same concerns, joys, and hopes for our families. And when asked what their dreams were, most often we heard them tell us how they desire a life of faith for their children.

God is at work in Haiti, through those willing to share what they have and through people like the dedicated staff of Compassion, who live and worship among those they serve.

Christ calls us to help those in need. There are so many ways to share our physical and spiritual wealth with those less fortunate, whether they are next door, in our own communities, or across the globe.

Bev

PRAY

God, help me to be sensitive to your direction as I share your love with a hurting world. Help me to love in both word and deed.

SAVOR

How can you live out the love of God not only in word but also in deed today?

Week 2, Day 7
I NEED YOU

He called a little child to him, and placed the child among them. And he said: "Truly I tell you, unless you change and become like little children, you will never enter the kingdom of heaven. —MATTHEW 18:2-3 (NIV)

One day many years ago, I drove my son to a birthday party for his friend who was turning four or five years old. It was the first time our son was invited to a birthday party without a parent coming along. On the way to the party, there was nothing but anticipation and excitement on his face.

I parked in front of the house and thought that he would just get out and go to the door of the house. But he hesitated and suddenly became very quiet. Then, out of the blue, he said, "Mommy, I need you to go to the door with me."

We went to the door, and he joined the party. When I got back to my car, it hit me: my little guy had just plainly told me that he needed me. I realized that the time would come when he would not need me anymore. So I tucked the memory into my heart, and it still moves me, all these years later.

I've thought about how sweet those same words must sound to my Father in heaven: I need you. No pretenses about being able to do it on my own. Does not God surely feel the same way as I did when my son told me he needed me? Would he not be happy to help when I ask?

I am reminded of an old hymn we sang at church: "I need Thee, O I need Thee / Every hour I need Thee / O bless me now, my Savior / I come to Thee."

My heart was warmed when my child told me that he needed me. God asks us to become as little children, and I'm certain that he is delighted when we are honest about our need for him.

Anneliese

PRAY

Dear Jesus, I need you now. Help me to be honest about my need for you every single day.

SAVOR

What is it that you need God to do today that will lighten your load? Tell him about it.

WEEK 3

Family Journeys
SOWING SEEDS FROM SUSANNA

Though my grandmother is long gone, I think of her often. It's the little things I remember, like shelling peas together and singing her favorite hymns. I have a few of her treasures, including her German Bible and her old Singer sewing machine, which spent many years in a shed on the prairie and which now sits proudly in my front entryway.

In one drawer of the sewing machine cabinet were two envelopes of seeds she had collected in 1957. A few years ago, I decided to plant the seeds in hopes of producing some heritage plants. I was so excited to see a few teeny green sprouts, and I watered them faithfully. One day, however, I realized those healthy young plants were shaped suspiciously like the weeds I was pulling from an adjacent garden bed.

Above: Susanna's sewing machine cabinet.

What a disappointment! My hope had been to grow a few of Grandma's flowers, save the seeds, and share them with all my sisters and cousins. But it was not to be. So instead I will share a few memories taken from her handwritten journal. Susanna Penner was born in 1893 in Rosenthal, Russia, the eighth daughter in the family. In her journal she tells of her school days, and of becoming a teacher in the village of Grigorjewka at the age of seventeen. She writes, "Here at Grigorjewka I met my husband, Johann Baerg. September 9, 1912 was our wedding day. The Scripture chosen for our marriage was Romans 12:12. . . . Be joyful in hope, patient in affliction, faithful in prayer. This verse was our theme through life!"

It's the little things I remember, like shelling peas together and singing her favorite hymns.

She continues, "This was a nice, peaceful time in Russia and we were happy and content. But not for long! When the First World War began, my husband was called to serve while I stayed at home alone with two small children. He was away for two years before the war ended and the Russian Revolution began. That was much worse than the war. The White Army took all the young men from our village with them, chasing them to the Caucasus and from there by ship to the Crimea. A few managed to hide and escape halfway through this

Judy's grandmother Susanna Penner Baerg, with her two oldest children in 1915.

journey. From these deserters I was able to learn that my husband had been sent to the Crimea. When he had been away for seven months, I gave birth to another son whose name was Jacob. When Jacob was one, his father returned home . . . sick, weak and on crutches. What a celebration!"

My grandmother goes on to tell of the difficult journey that took the family from their beloved home in Russia to Canada. She shares of the hardships and joys of life in her new country and how God gave strength for each day. As she neared the end of her life, she penned these words: "The Lord allows these sorrows, but also helps us to bear the pain . . . therefore I love the Lord!"

Though I may not have my grandmother's seeds to pass along, I am thankful for the words she penned, and for her unwavering trust in God.

Judy

Recipe
BORSCHT

Yields about 10 quarts / 9.5 L

Stock
- 1 chuck roast or 7-bone roast, rinsed and patted dry
- Salt and pepper
- 1 onion, cut in half
- 1–3 celery stalks (with leaves), cut in half
- 2–3 carrots, cut in half
- 2 bay leaves
- 5–10 peppercorns

1. In a large (11-quart / 10.5-L) pot, season roast with salt and pepper, and sear on all sides.
2. Cover the seared meat with water. Add all the remaining stock ingredients and bring to a boil. Lower heat to simmer. Simmer until roast is fork tender. This could take 2–4 hours.
3. Remove roast from pot, place in an oven-safe pan, and set aside. Strain the stock, discarding the stock vegetables. If you added soup

bones (see tip), you can return them to the broth along with the vegetables, then take them out when the soup is ready to serve.

4. While stock is simmering, prepare soup ingredients.

Soup

- 1 onion, diced
- 1 bell pepper, diced
- 2–3 celery stalks, diced
- 1 jalapeño pepper, diced (optional)
- 2–3 potatoes, peeled, diced, and divided
- 1–2 tablespoons / 15–30 ml vegetable oil
- 2 (15-ounce / 425-g) cans stewed tomatoes, blended
- 1 head green cabbage, cored and cut into thin shreds
- 3 carrots, grated
- 1 (8-ounce / 225-g) can tomato sauce
- 1 (15-ounce / 425-g) can garbanzo beans, rinsed and drained (optional)
- Small bunch dill, or more to taste, chopped
- 1 handful Italian parsley, chopped
- 1 teaspoon / 5 ml salt
- ½ teaspoon / 2 ml pepper
- Sour cream, to garnish

1. In a large pan, sauté onion, pepper, celery, jalapeño (if desired), and one of the diced potatoes in vegetable oil.

2. When these ingredients are soft, blend them in a blender with stewed tomatoes. Depending on the size of your blender, you might need to do this in batches. Be careful with the hot ingredients.

3. Add this mixture to the prepared stock (above). Add the remaining ingredients.

4. Bring to a boil, then lower the heat and simmer until all the vegetables are done.

5. While the soup is simmering, season the roast well with salt and pepper and heat in a 325° F / 160° C degree oven to serve alongside the *Borscht*. Serve *Borscht* with a dollop of sour cream, slices of the prepared roast, and good bread.

There are many versions of *Borscht*. Our family and relatives pronounce *Borscht* without the *t* sound at the end: *Borsch*. Our family and relatives lived in small villages in Russia and would be considered peasants, who used what they grew for food. This is a long process if you cook the stock and soup in one day. Start early in the day if you are making your own beef stock. I love *Borscht* today, but when I was young I could not tolerate eating it; I did not enjoy the many textures in the soup, especially the cabbage. My mother always made her *Borscht* with cabbage instead of beets. This is my mother's recipe, which she tweaked over the years, adding jalapeño to the recipe when she was eighty years old.

TIP

If you can't find a roast with the bones, buy two or three soup bones from the butcher to add along with the roast.

Ellen

Week 3, Day 1
GOD THE KNITTER

*As far as the east is from the west, so far does he remove
our transgressions from us.* —PSALM 103:12 (ESV)

I have always enjoyed knitting. I have memories of being a little girl sitting on a small chair beside my mother, being so proud that I was knitting just like her.

Recently, I was knitting a scarf using a lovely designer yarn I had purchased on impulse while enjoying a day's outing with my girlfriends. I was making up my own pattern, and it involved some trial and error. Trying to remember and follow the stitch pattern in my head, I made some mistakes that forced me to unravel my work. I had to unravel it to a point all the way below the mistake before I could resume knitting my project. My thoughts fell into rhythm with the click of the needles, and I thought about the differences between knitting and sewing.

Having been a seamstress for many years, I think I have seen just about every kind of damage that can be done to a garment. I have patched, camouflaged, and repaired all kinds of problems to restore garments as close to "as good as new" as I could. But even when a seamstress does her best work, it always remains clear that a sewn garment has been patched.

So often our forgiveness as humans is like that, isn't it? We forgive one another, but we only "patch things up." The seam is still visible. We remember and know exactly where the patch is.

But with knitting, a mistake does not damage the garment. The offending stitches are simply undone and the knitting continues. After the repair, no one could ever know that a mistake had been made because the garment is perfect.

That is what God's forgiveness is like. When we come to God with our sin and ask him to forgive us, God doesn't put a patch over it. He actually unravels the mistake, picks up the stitches of our life, and resumes knitting as though the mistake had never been made.

Aren't you thankful God knits rather than sews?

Julie

PRAY

God, thank you for removing my sin and making me whole and complete again.

SAVOR

What sin do you need to ask God to unravel and knit again today?

THE AROMA OF SELFLESS SERVING

*Then Mary took about a pint of pure nard, an expensive perfume;
she poured it on Jesus' feet and wiped his feet with her hair. And the
house was filled with the fragrance of the perfume.* —JOHN 12:3 (NIV)

One Saturday morning I rushed around, watching the clock, timing out what had to be finished. I was looking for the details to be perfect. Special. It mattered to me.

I had invited my beloved's mom, aunts, and cousin over for lunch. They had requested that we get together so that I could sign a few cookbooks for them. Their suggestion was to meet at a local restaurant. I had agreed at first, and then felt that a visit at home would be more conducive to conversation and relaxation, so I invited them to our home.

The weekend seemed so busy already. Did it really matter if we met in a restaurant? It would have made my life easier.

Reprioritizing the weekend made it all worthwhile. Laying the table with a freshly pressed tablecloth and my prettiest dishes while taking the morning to put together some fresh ingredients relaxed me and prepared my heart.

I silently thanked the Lord for the opportunity to have these special ladies in our home. I felt they deserved to feel that an effort had been made on their behalf. Instead of feeling stressed and frustrated, I felt peaceful. I knew that it mattered. My motives were honest, and God was okay with my rushing and hurrying.

They came. We shared a simple meal together. We looked at photos together. We talked about family and those we missed. As they left, I already looked forward to having them over again.

What good is a warm and comfortable bungalow if I don't open our door? My desire was to provide a setting in which conversation would flow with memories and laughter. It took some time and creativity, but ultimately I think it fed our souls. In the rush of it all, God prepared my heart.

Lovella

PRAY

Lord, help me to open my home and my heart to demonstrate your love.

SAVOR

To whom could you show love through a warm welcome and a beautifully laid table?

Week 3, Day 3

COINCIDENCE?

Therefore confess your sins to each other and pray for each other so that you may be healed. The prayer of a righteous person is powerful and effective. —JAMES 5:16 (NIV)

A number of years ago, my husband was out of town on a business trip and I was home by myself. As I got ready for bed that night, I felt a great fear come over me. I grabbed my Bible and opened it at random to James 5:16. The last part of the verse assured me that "the prayer of a righteous person is powerful and effective."

Next I picked up a devotional book, and the devotion for the day was based on James 5:16. I got goosebumps, and I felt God's peace begin to flow through me. After spending some more time reading the Bible and praying, I was still in awe of how God had sent this verse to me twice.

Then, after I put down the devotional book, I picked up a novel that I was reading. After I read a few pages, James 5:16 popped up again! For the third time!

I smiled and said, "Okay, God; I get it." Coincidence? No way. There is no doubt in my mind that God heard me and took the fear from me. As I fell asleep that night, I had peace!

It is easy to take note when huge things happen in our lives and we see God's answers to our prayers. But we know that God is listening to our hearts even in the little things. When he doesn't answer according to our plan, we tend to think that our prayers haven't been answered. But when we pray in faith, God hears us, and he answers in the best way for us.

That night, God answered my little prayer in a way that left no doubt that he had heard me. Let's remember to trust God for answers in the little things as well as the big ones.

PRAY

Lord, help me to trust you in large and small things. Thank you for answering my prayers.

SAVOR

When have you called something a coincidence that might have been God's work in the little things?

Week 3, Day 4
WHY TO WHO

We have this hope as an anchor for the soul, firm and secure. It enters the inner sanctuary behind the curtain, where our forerunner, Jesus, has entered on our behalf. —HEBREWS 6:19-20 (NIV)

In the past few months, we have walked through tough times with several of our close friends.

My first inclination, upon hearing difficult news, is to ask, "Why, Lord? Why do these friends have to go through this loss, this crisis, that terrible situation? Why?"

At the funeral for the daughter of some good friends, the pastor reminded us that the question is not *why* but *who*. Who can we call on in times of trouble? Who loves us more than we can imagine? Who knows what we are feeling right now? Who is walking with us all along the way?

The answer to all of these questions is God. God alone can be trusted. He alone is in control. Without God, there are no answers to the hard questions, no reasons for difficult times, and, worst of all, no hope.

In my devotions over the past few weeks, the theme of hope reappeared time and again. "For everything that was written in the past was written to teach us, so that through the endurance taught in the Scriptures and the encouragement they provide we might have hope" (Romans 15:4 NIV). "May the God of hope fill you with all joy and peace as you trust in him, so that you may overflow with hope by the power of the Holy Spirit" (Romans 15:13 NIV). These verses from Romans and the passage above from Hebrews assure us that we have a hope that anchors our souls securely.

In the valley of the shadow of death in which we sometimes live, the *why* questions may never go away entirely. But when we begin to ask *who* instead, we can have absolute confidence in the answer.

Bev

Week 3, Day 5

FEAR OR FAITH?

Now faith is confidence in what we hope for and assurance about what we do not see. —HEBREWS 11:1 (NIV)

Have you ever said "I will believe it when I see it"? This is the response I often receive when I relate the story of a sea lion that came to visit us on our farm one summer. We live about one hundred kilometers from the ocean and many kilometers from the nearest river, so people's skepticism is understandable. But it seems that sea lions can navigate their way up drainage ditches!

But God says just the opposite: we will see it when we believe it. That's quite a reversal! God invites us to believe before we can see anything. True faith is finding certainty in uncertain territory. We step forward . . . toward what is not fully known or seen. That is why it is called faith.

We can't see what the road ahead looks like. In fact, it may look as if we are stepping off at the deep end. But faith is visualizing the future. It's believing something before it can be seen. Faith is that first step into the unseen. As we move forward, we will see God open the way.

Hebrews 11 gives us so many wonderful examples of people who had faith and stepped out into the unknown. Abraham, Sarah, Jacob, Moses: these and others conquered their fear and walked forward in faith. They believed before they saw any evidence.

If you are like me, fear often wins over faith. Here's the challenge for me and maybe for you too: start moving even if I can't see what lies ahead, and trust God!

Judy

Week 3, Day 6
KEEP THE DRESS

Know therefore that the Lord your God is God; he is the faithful God, keeping his covenant of love to a thousand generations of those who love him and keep his commandments. —DEUTERONOMY 7:9 (NIV)

A few years ago while I was on a cleaning binge, I discovered my mother's wedding dress in a closet. Her own mother, my grandmother, had carefully sewn it. Its creamy lace skirt and satin bodice spoke of a bygone era, as did the wedding veil that went with it.

I called my sister to see if she would like to keep the dress. We had almost decided to give it to a thrift store when my sister suddenly blurted out: "No . . . wait! We can't get rid of this dress. This dress means commitment!"

We knew our mother had worked hard and had stayed loyal and committed to her marriage. Her life was not without challenges. But a good marriage is not something you find; it's something that you work for. A good marriage takes struggle. At times you need to confront, and at other times you need to confess. The practice of forgiveness is essential.

Today's media has rediscovered the word *commitment* but turned it into an optional plan. "Happily ever after" has been transformed into "Make me happy . . . or I'll find someone who will!"

What is real commitment? We can look to God for the answer. God didn't choose you because you were beautiful or successful or popular. God chose you out of sheer love, and God keeps his covenant to you. What a model of commitment for our own marriages!

So we decided to keep our mother's wedding dress. It's a symbol of the commitment of our parents, and a symbol of God's commitment to us. Let's honor the call to holiness rather than to happiness. Let's water our marriages with an unwavering commitment to please God above everything else.

Keep the dress. Revisit your vows. And say "I do"—to your spouse and to God—every single day.

PRAY

God, strengthen my commitment to my marriage vows. Thank you for modeling commitment for us.

SAVOR

What two things can you do to "keep the dress" today? What small actions can you take to remind yourself and your spouse of your marriage vows?

Week 3, Day 7
SABBATH REST

Come to me, all you who are weary and burdened, and I will give you rest. Take my yoke upon you and learn from me, for I am gentle and humble in heart, and you will find rest for your souls. For my yoke is easy and my burden is light. —MATTHEW 11:28-30 (NIV)

I grew up in a home in which Sundays were completely different from any other day of the week. We went to church, came home, and had a relaxed family dinner. Mom and Dad took naps, and we could play until friends came over, and then play some more. We were not allowed to do homework.

Now, I know that this might sound legalistic. And the rules were indeed clear. But at the same time, these rules were so freeing. The rules forced us to work ahead, and then we were able to enjoy a free day.

We read in the Gospels how the "law-abiding" Pharisees were quick to judge Jesus of working on the Sabbath when he healed someone or picked grains in the field. Jesus set out to explain that "the Sabbath was made for man, not man for the Sabbath" (Mark 2:27 NIV).

Simply stated, Jesus was telling them that the Sabbath rest was created for our good, not to make life difficult with rules and restraints.

In this fast-paced way of life we live, where we do not need to plan ahead because everything is available around the clock, it is harder to set aside a day of rest. But maybe we need to consider how to plan ahead so we can slow down, take time to listen, worship, invite someone for coffee, play, take the kids to the park, or read a book.

We may be surprised at what we can accomplish when we are rested and recharged, because ultimately our Creator knows what we need.

Anneliese

PRAY

God, give me the grace to slow down and rest at your feet. Help me to find my true rest in you.

SAVOR

What do your Sundays look like? What "rules" might you put in place to help you find rest for your soul on that day or another day during the week?

WEEK 4

Family Journeys
A VILLAGE ABLAZE

One night in November 1976, my siblings and I gathered around our grandfather as he shared about a difficult time in his life. This is some of what he shared.

Henry Abram Regehr was born in Muensterberg, Russia. He was the youngest of twelve children who were brought up in a godly home. At the age of fourteen, he accepted the Lord Jesus as his own personal Savior.

On the night of November 19, 1919, his peaceful home life was forever changed when revolutionary bandits came through their village. Grandpa was sixteen years old when this happened. By the time the dastardly deeds of that night were finished, our grandfather had

Above: Kathy's grandparents, Tina and Henry Regehr, with their eldest daughter, Katie, just before they left Russia.

witnessed the killing of his parents. He lost eighteen members of his family that night.

He told how in those moments, it seemed a voice was telling him to run. He jumped through a window into the cold, dark uncertainty of night. Running barefoot through the garden, he turned to see his home and village ablaze, a sign that the bandits were finished and moving on to the next village.

It was at this point in his story that he told us, his grandchildren, that he would not say any more about the cruelty of that night. It is hardly understandable for those who have not lived through such a time. He believed God would help, but how?

His story did not end there. As an orphan, he became dependent upon the hospitality of his married siblings, who provided him with a home in Blumendorf. By the higher hand of God, his life had been spared. Times were difficult, and the revolution was followed by a famine. He, along with his siblings, worked hard to rebuild their lives and futures.

It seemed a voice was telling him to run. He jumped through a window into the cold, dark uncertainty of night. He believed God would help, but how?

I'll never forget how his eyes lit up when he said, "I lived with my brother Abraham until I found the very best and only girl for me, a nice flower. I was twenty-one years old when Tina Warkentin and I were married. Our lives together started and surely a new chapter in my life had also begun. Life seemed to take on a new meaning, and the future was something to plan for and look forward to."

On May 17, 1927, my grandparents, along with their eldest daughter, immigrated to Canada. They arrived in Steinbach, Manitoba, and ten days later moved to Foam Lake, Saskatchewan, where my mom and three more children were born. In 1948, they moved back to Steinbach, where he was self-employed, and where he later pastored a church.

Our grandfather told us this story on the day of our grandparents' fifty-third wedding anniversary. As his story came to a close, he reminded us that it is better to trust in the Lord than to put confidence in humans. He bowed and gave thanks before our great God in praise and thanksgiving.

As the psalmist writes, "I called upon the Lord in distress:

Kathy's grandfather Henry Abram Regehr after he moved his family to Foam Lake, Saskatchewan.

The Lord answered me, and set me in a large place. The Lord is on my side; I will not fear: what can man do unto me?" (Psalm 118:56 KJV).

Kathy

Recipe
BREAD AND BUTTER PICKLES

Yields 8 cups / 2 L

- Long English cucumbers, enough to almost fill a 1-gallon / 4-L container when sliced
- 2 cups / 500 ml sweet white onions

1. Using a mandoline or knife, thinly slice cucumbers and onions into 1-gallon / 4-L container. Set aside while you make the brine.

Brine

- 4 cups / 1 L white sugar
- 2 tablespoons / 30 ml pickling salt
- 1 teaspoon / 5 ml turmeric
- 1 teaspoon / 5 ml celery seed
- 1 teaspoon / 5 ml mustard seed
- 2 cups / 500 ml white vinegar

1. Measure all brine ingredients into a pot and bring to a boil. Turn down the heat and simmer for 2–3 minutes.
2. Pour hot brine over sliced cucumbers and onions.
3. Stir and allow to cool on counter. Once cool, cover and place in refrigerator.
4. Stir every few days. Pickles are best after sitting in brine for about 1 week.

Summer-fresh cucumbers and onions make the best pickles. These no-fuss pickles are delicious served on the side or in a sandwich.

TIP

Several days after making these pickles, I like to transfer them into glass jars. I find they keep better in glass, and glass jars make them easier to store and serve. Like any pickles, these keep well for a long time in the refrigerator.

Kathy

Week 4, Day 1
TAKE CARE OF THE SMALL THINGS

---

*"In your anger do not sin": Do not let the sun go down
while you are still angry.* —**EPHESIANS 4:26 (NIV)**

When I opened my freezer recently, I was surprised to see a big crack in the pail that held blended strawberries that I had prepared for jam. When I had poured the thick liquid into the container on that summer day a few months earlier, I had noticed a short crack right at the top—just over an inch long. But since the liquid did not go up to the crack, I had figured it would be fine. I had simply closed the lid and stored it away for a winter cooking day.

What I had not taken into account was how the pressure of the mixture, freezing and expanding, would cause the crack to grow. Now I had a mess on my hands.

I immediately thought about a sermon I had just heard on how small disagreements can cause great friction when under pressure, disrupting the unity we have in the faith. In Philippians 4:2, the apostle Paul pleads with Euodia and with Syntyche to agree with each other in the Lord. Why would Paul beg them so? He knew the harm that their disunity would do to their growth and witness.

As believers and partakers in the grace of our Lord Jesus Christ, we want to follow his example and be gentle and forgiving toward one another. Our witness is squelched when we argue and fight. Jesus said, "By this everyone will know that you are my disciples, if you love one another" (John 13:35 NIV).

This broken pail has become a vivid reminder for me to take care of small things before they become big issues. Taking the time to work out the small disagreements with care and sensitivity will pay off down the road and will keep us whole in Christ.

Anneliese

PRAY

God, help me to deal with the small things in my family and my friendships.

SAVOR

What small things plague your relationships? How might you take one step toward dealing with them today?

Week 4, Day 2
LISTEN

He says, "Be still, and know that I am God; I will be exalted among the nations, I will be exalted in the earth. —**PSALM 46:10 (NIV)**

Recently I received a call from my sister when she just needed to talk. Shortly into the call she said, "Thanks for listening to me." It made me remember how many times she has been the one on the other end of the phone listening to me.

Soon after that, a very dear friend called and we had a long conversation. We both talked about what was on our hearts, and at the end of our conversation, she said, "Thank you for listening." Again I thought about the many times she has been the one who gave the gift of listening to me.

My husband and I once took a course at our church called "Hearing God." As I worked through the homework for this course, I realized how important it is for me to be still and listen to the voice of God.

God has a personal message for each of us. He loves each of us, and desires that we take time to be still. I am so grateful for the many times I have come to him, knowing he always listens. Like a good friend on the other end of the line, God is listening to what I say.

Now I must also ask: Am I listening to God? The desire of my heart is to glorify God by listening to him. When I do, my life will be transformed into his likeness. When I do, God's response will be "Thank you for listening to me."

Kathy

PRAY

Thank you, God, for listening to me. Help me to also listen to you.

SAVOR

What do you want to tell God today? Take a moment to also listen for him.

Week 4, Day 3
NEWBORNS

---

*"For I know the plans I have for you," declares the Lord, "plans
to prosper you and not to harm you, plans to give you hope and a
future." —*JEREMIAH 29:11 (NIV)

The gift of a newborn can bring such joy into our lives. Oh, how
my spirit rejoiced each time I heard the wonderful news that we
were going to be parents! I remember those early days of parenthood
as if they happened yesterday: staring down at the innocent and perfect face of our sleeping newborn child, being filled with awe at God's
marvelous creation, and praying for God's blessing upon that new life.
Within each child lives a world of possibilities from God.

Sadly, not all new life happens under ideal circumstances. For
twenty years I volunteered with our local crisis pregnancy center as a
crisis line counselor, and I heard the stories of women and men who
found themselves in desperate situations, needing support in dealing
with their pregnancies. We can't understand why some children grow
up feeling unloved and neglected. We ask why a child is born with
serious health concerns or why a baby or child who was wanted and

prayed for suddenly dies. These questions can leave us feeling deep sadness and helplessness. But God is the creator of all life, regardless of circumstances. Every birth reminds us that life itself is a miracle.

As a mother, I know that the love a parent has for a child is incredibly powerful, and that the desire to protect, guard, and nurture that child is immense. But God's love is far more powerful than even a parent's love. The Lord has placed intrinsic value and hope in each person, in newborn life and in your life as well.

Life is vulnerable, fragile, and precious. Ask yourself: What difference can I make in someone's life? We can walk alongside another in both good and difficult times and whisper gently, lovingly, "God loves you. God has a wonderful plan for you, with hope for your future. Trust in the God of hope; he alone is sovereign."

Charlotte

Week 4, Day 4
READ IT—AND DO IT!

Do not merely listen to the word, and so deceive yourselves. Do what it says. —JAMES 1:22 (NIV)

Recently I have been sorting through all the boxes in our crawl space. We've lived in the same house for almost forty years, and things have really accumulated down there! It was time to review, reduce, and recycle.

One day as I was rooting through boxes, I came across a number of Bibles. I found my husband's and my first Bibles, presented to us by our parents when we were very young. I found his parents' family Bible, his mom's *Living Bible*, a German Bible published in the early 1900s, plus several more.

Seeing all these Bibles reminded me of the importance of this book in my walk with God.

The next morning in church, the speaker told a story that challenged me. A missionary shared Jesus with a man in his home village in Laos. The man prayed to receive Christ, and they were both joyful.

Unfortunately, the missionary had to leave that same day. So the man asked the missionary, "What do I do now?" The missionary asked him if he could read. When the man said yes, the missionary gave him a Bible. "Start reading in John," the missionary said, "and do it."

The man did just that. Two years later, the missionary returned and met this man again. In that short time, the man had led eight hundred people in his village to Christ.

That is the Christian walk in a nutshell: Pick up God's Word. Read it—and do it!

Bev

I AM THE VINE

Abide in me, and I in you. As the branch cannot bear fruit by itself, unless it abides in the vine, neither can you, unless you abide in me. I am the vine; you are the branches. Whoever abides in me and I in him, it is that bears much fruit, for apart from me you can do nothing. —JOHN 15:4-5 (ESV)

A few years ago we planted our first grapevines. They are mostly an experiment. We are hoping there will be some fruit in the years ahead that our grandkids will enjoy. They are always interested in what is growing in our garden.

Looking at our new grapevines, I couldn't help but think of Jesus talking about being the vine. He is not one of the vines, but *the* vine. This rich imagery from the gospel of John reminds us of our connection to Jesus, the source of our nourishment and life.

What does it mean to abide in Christ? It is a choice we can make to spend time in prayer, reading the Bible, and focusing on Christ.

We cannot bear fruit in our lives apart from a connection to the vine. Any good fruit we bear will be Christ's work in our lives and not something we ourselves have produced. If we neglect to nourish our relationship with Christ, our faith will struggle. We'll lack wisdom in the choices we make, and our lives will reflect that.

The good news is that fruit is the natural result of abiding in Christ. It is through God's grace that we are able to have a relationship with Christ that transforms our lives and hearts. Because he loved us first, we love him and want to spend time with him. We can be confident that the work that God began in us will be completed and we will be found faithful.

Lorella

PRAY

Jesus, thank you for being the true vine. Root my life in you, and help me to bear fruit today.

SAVOR

What would it look like for you to "abide in Christ" this week?

Week 4, Day 6
DON'T FORGET

When you have eaten and are satisfied, praise the Lord your God for the good land he has given you. Be careful that you do not forget the Lord your God, failing to observe his commands, his laws and his decrees that I am giving you this day. —DEUTERONOMY 8:10-11 (NIV)

After losing her husband and two children in Russia, my grandmother fled to Germany with one young son, my father. He told us how he had to look for food in trash cans.

It's no wonder my father would never allow us to complain at the table. If we fussed or found fault with the meal, it was just cause to send us away from the table. He knew both the pain of hunger and the blessing of having a table before him filled with food.

Today, we live in a land of plenty, boasting flowing wheat fields, wineries, orchards, dairy, and poultry farms. The city where I live happens to be one of the berry capitals of the world. No matter the season, we can find almost any ingredient to make delicious meals, snacks, and desserts. Yes, we have much more than we need.

Although these verses from Deuteronomy are God's words to the people of Israel, I can't help but think how they apply to me. Having heard about the hardships my father faced and how God brought him to this country, I think it may be easy for the next generations to take what we have for granted—or worse, to forget about God. Psalm 62:10 tells us "though your riches increase, do not set your heart on them" (NIV).

When I read these words, I feel like I am lovingly warned not to hold onto material things, but to God, who has given us all things. Whatever our past, today it comes down to remembering our salvation and ultimately what we have been saved from.

I want to remember to give thanks, lest I forget that it is the Lord God who gives.

Anneliese

PRAY

Lord Jesus, you are the giver of all good things. Help me never forget the ways that you are the source of everything good in my life.

SAVOR

How do you maintain a grateful spirit and remain mindful of God, even in the midst of plenty?

Week 4, Day 7
HOTEL GUEST OR NURSE?

If I then, your Lord and Teacher, have washed your feet, you also ought to wash one another's feet. For I have given you an example, that you also should do just as I have done to you. Truly, truly, I say to you, a servant is not greater than his master, nor is a messenger greater than the one who sent him. If you know these things, blessed are you if you do them. —JOHN 13:14-17 (ESV)

A few week ago a speaker at our church asked us to evaluate whether our day-to-day attitude about life is more like that of a guest at a hotel or that of a nurse at a hospital.

This is a relevant challenge to me at this time because my husband and I have been traveling and staying in hotels. Also, it's the time of year for my annual medical checkups. During these appointments, I see nurses working to make things comfortable for me and serve my needs.

Hotel guests want everything provided for them: clean room, fresh linens, fresh towels, a lovely bed. They want the hotel to provide any other luxuries as needed. Hotel guests are very disappointed when they don't receive everything they expect.

A nurse, on the other hand, looks to the needs of others. A nurse provides what the patient needs. A nurse may have to change bedpans or perform other undesirable tasks. A nurse does what the doctor orders.

So am I a hotel guest or a nurse? Do I demand things of life and others around me, expecting that I'll be given the best treatment and the most attention? Or do I have a nurse's heart: one that looks to the needs of others and that is willing to serve? Jesus encouraged his disciples to be like nurses, who serve others and wash their feet.

I've been challenged to consider my attitude toward those around me. Am I more like a demanding hotel guest or a self-giving nurse?

Ellen

PRAY

Lord Jesus, help me to approach others with the desire to help and bless. Give me a servant's heart.

SAVOR

When have you acted more like a hotel guest in life than like a nurse? How can you operate out of a servant's heart today?

WEEK 5

Family Journeys
OUR LEADER? THE LORD GOD!

My *Oma* (grandma), Liese Neufeld, had an unusually vivacious personality, especially so when compared to her peers. I did not learn half of her story until after she passed away. A short look into her childhood through the eyes of her brother, my great-uncle, demonstrates how things were in Russia after World War I, and also how God was still at work in a country where God was not welcome.

My grandmother's family lived in the kind of farmhouse in which the barn was attached to the house so that in winter it was easier to tend to the livestock. Her mother usually had one or two maids, and her father also had a stablehand. During the time of the Makhno

Above: Anneliese's grandparents, Liese (Neufeld) and Heinrich Friesen, on their wedding day in Paraguay in January 1934.

bandits, her father's life was threatened several times in their own home. All religious teaching was banned, and a plaque put up at their school stated "Heaven and earth will pass away, but my words will not pass away. —Lenin."

The children had to be very careful not to talk about any religious activity in their homes; if they did, their parents could be taken away, as a lot of spying was going on. It was during this time, however, that my grandmother's parents gave their lives to God and were baptized.

In November 1929, the family of thirteen left for the train station at dusk. Their longtime stablehand drove them to the station, and they gave him the wagons and horses as a token of their thanks.

At this time there were about fifteen thousand people gathered in Moscow, trying to leave the country. Alarmed at the influx of people, a government official asked one elderly Mennonite woman if she could tell him who their leader was. She replied, "Certainly! It is the dear Lord God; no other!" Upon hearing this, the commissioner spat and sent her away.

> *A government official asked one elderly*
> *Mennonite woman who their leader was.*
> *She replied, "It is the dear Lord God; no other!"*

Thousands were sent back to their homes, and many were never heard from again. However, a delegation diligently sought to get help from Germany, and eventually they received permission and help to leave.

After some time in a refugee camp in Germany, my grandmother and her family emigrated, some older siblings to Canada and the rest of them with their parents to Paraguay. My grandmother, as a sixteen-year-old, went to Paraguay. A three-week journey by ship took them to South America. A large riverboat then took them to the Chaco, where they were dropped off in a barren, mosquito- and snake-infested land to begin a new life.

It amazes me to think that despite the hard pioneering labor, weddings and births and happy times still abounded. Oma married in January 1934, and my mother was born in December of that year. Sadly, my grandfather died in 1948 due to complications from a well-digging accident, leaving Liese widowed with six children.

My grandmother married again after his death, this time to a man who had also fled Russia. My step-grandfather later found out that his wife and children, from whom he had been separated during the war and who had been declared dead, were still alive in Russia. Another hurdle to work through and overcome!

By the time I was born and got to know these grandparents, I never would have guessed the hardships they had faced. Oma always had a twinkle in her eyes, and my step-grandfather was just the best Opa around.

Anneliese

Recipe
MACARONI AND CHEESE

Serves 8

- 3 cups / 750 ml elbow macaroni, uncooked
- ¼ cup / 60 ml butter
- ⅓ cup / 75 ml flour
- ½ cup / 125 ml onion, minced
- 2 cloves garlic, minced
- 4 cups / 1 L whole milk
- 1 teaspoon / 5 ml salt
- 1 tablespoon / 15 ml Dijon-style mustard
- ¼ teaspoon / 1 ml cayenne pepper (optional)
- 1 jalapeño pepper, finely minced (optional)
- 4 cups / 1 L sharp cheddar cheese, shredded and divided
- 1 cup / 250 ml cottage cheese

Topping

- 1 cup / 250 ml panko (Japanese bread crumbs)
- ⅓ cup / 75 ml Parmesan cheese, grated
- 2 tablespoons / 30 ml butter, melted

1. Bring a large pot of water to a boil. Add 1 tablespoon / 15 ml salt.
2. Add macaroni and cook 6 minutes, or until just tender. (The macaroni will continue to cook and absorb sauce later as it bakes.) Drain, rinse, and set aside.
3. In a large saucepan, melt the butter over medium heat.
4. Use a wooden spoon to stir in the flour, onion, and garlic. Continue to cook, stirring constantly until the flour mixture is cooked and just begins to color.
5. Add a little milk, stir until smooth, and repeat, until all the milk has been added. Whisk over medium heat until the white sauce is bubbly and has thickened. Stir in 1 teaspoon / 5 ml salt and mustard.
6. Add optional items—cayenne pepper and jalapeño pepper—if you want to add some zip.
7. Remove the sauce from heat, add 3 cups / 750 ml cheddar cheese and cottage cheese, and stir to combine. Add cooked macaroni.
8. Turn into a 9 x 13-inch / 23 x 33-cm greased casserole dish or individual baking dishes.

9. Sprinkle with remaining 1 cup / 250 ml cheddar cheese.
10. For topping, combine breadcrumbs with Parmesan cheese and melted butter. Sprinkle over the macaroni and cheese.
11. Bake uncovered in a 400° F / 205° C oven about 30 minutes, or until crumbs are toasted and macaroni and cheese is bubbly around the edges.

Macaroni and cheese is comfort food at its best. We love any kind of pasta at our house. While macaroni and cheese is considered a splurge, we enjoy this treat occasionally, and we are thankful for local farmers who provide us with excellent dairy products.

TIPS

When you buy the cheese, you will need a total of 1 pound / 450 g to make 4 cups / 1 L of shredded cheese. A combination of cheddar and Monterey Jack or cheddar and Gruyère also works well.

Baking the macaroni and cheese in a shallow dish gives each bite a bit of crispy topping.

Lovella

Week 5, Day 1

LESSONS OF A HUMMINGBIRD

And no creature is hidden from his sight, but all are naked and exposed to the eyes of him to whom we must give account. —HEBREWS 4:13 (ESV)

We have hummingbird feeders hanging just outside our kitchen window so that we can watch the entertaining hummingbirds as we enjoy our meals. One morning I commented to my husband, "I wish I could be a different animal each day: a dolphin one day, a rabbit the next, then a hummingbird."

My husband chuckled at me and suggested that I would need to be careful to be able to come back and not get stuck in an animal body. I smiled, but I continued on. "We can watch the behavior of each animal, and predict what it will do, but we can't truly understand how they think or reason, can we?"

My husband agreed that there wasn't a way to know this. "So the only way we could truly know is to become a hummingbird ourselves," I replied.

What relevance this has to what God did for us! A God-being, the Creator of all things, having a mind that surpasses anything we might understand or grasp—how can such a God truly understand who we are or what it is like to live in our physical bodies?

There is only one way. God was able to do what I cannot. I cannot take on the body of a hummingbird and experience its life. But God took on the physical body of a man and lived his life. So we can never say that God does not understand us. He does. He came down and became one of us!

Julie

Week 5, Day 2
AN OPEN DOOR

Therefore, as we have opportunity, let us do good to all. —GALATIANS 6:10 (NIV)

During the forty years that we have lived in our home, our neighbors have influenced our lives. We've watched our families grow, helped with babysitting, brought baked goods, and shared meals and garden produce. We've moved each other's pianos, started each other's cars, mowed each other's lawns, collected each other's mail, and gone looking for each other's wandering children and pets. We've wept with those who have experienced loss and rejoiced with those who were celebrating.

Jesus was a prime example of someone who was involved in his community. He showed compassion to those who were sick and wept with those who had lost family members. He often went out of his way to lighten burdens. He showed hospitality, using what was available. He blessed children with love and attention. He invited friends and strangers to join him in his God-given tasks.

Jesus also made himself vulnerable by asking for and receiving help from friends and strangers alike. So often we as Christians think that we should be the strong ones who help others, and we do not allow our neighbors the opportunity to help us. I learned this lesson many years ago when we couldn't find our then six-year-old son after school one day. We were frantic and called our neighbor, a single father, to help us look for him. He willingly came to our aid, and after a concentrated search, he was the one who found our son. He told me later that it blessed him so much to be asked to help. We had helped him on numerous occasions, but this experience told him that we trusted him and valued his help.

Let's be deliberate about opening our doors to friends and strangers. Let's offer friendship and encouragement to those who enter and help to those in need. And we shouldn't hesitate to knock on our neighbors' doors when we need help. Sometimes our vulnerability is exactly what is needed to build community.

Bev

PRAY

God, thank you for neighbors. Give me strength to help them and to ask for help when I need it.

SAVOR

What one thing could you do this week to build community in your neighborhood?

Week 5, Day 3
CLEAN

*Cleanse me with hyssop, and I will be clean; wash me, and I will be
whiter than snow. Let me hear joy and gladness; let the bones you
have crushed rejoice. Hide your face from my sins and blot out all my
iniquity. Create in me a pure heart, O God, and renew a steadfast
spirit within me.* —**PSALM 51:7-10 (NIV)**

One of the simple things in life for which I keep giving thanks is
a private, hot shower. Maybe I've read too many books about
hostages or inmates who don't have this convenience. Or maybe I am
reminded of the children I saw floating on shacks along the banks of
the muddy rivers in Indonesia.

I don't know about you, but these types of images make me appreciate something I would not want to live without. There is nothing
like soap and clean, warm water after working up a sweat or getting
chilled while walking in the rain. There is nothing like the wonderful
feeling of being clean again.

There is another kind of feeling clean that is even better, though. I
can hardly live with myself when I know I've grieved the heart of God.

Sin strains relationships and keeps us from experiencing peace. So on a spiritual level, I also need cleansing and refreshing.

In Psalm 51 the psalmist writes, "Wash me, and I will be whiter than snow." And in Psalm 32 he writes, "Oh, what joy for those whose disobedience is forgiven, whose sin is put out of sight!" (v. 1 NLT).

Being forgiven by God and those we have wronged is the best kind of feeling clean. Sometimes I wonder why it takes me so long to humble myself to ask forgiveness. There is nothing quite as wonderful as a restored relationship!

Let us not drag along our sacks of unforgiven sins anymore. Instead, let's leave them at the cross and allow the blood of Jesus to wash us whiter than snow.

Anneliese

PRAY
God, thank you for washing me clean in your presence. Help me to accept your forgiveness.

SAVOR
What relationship do you want to restore back to health? How can you begin to do that?

Week 5, Day 4

JOY COMES IN THE MORNING

Be joyful in hope, patient in affliction, faithful in prayer. —ROMANS 12:12 (NIV)

Years ago, we discovered a very large lymph node in our oldest son's neck. After a round of biopsies, we were told that he had Hodgkin's disease. Eventually the doctors decided that this had been a misdiagnosis. Thank God!

But by this time, I was in my own nightmare of anxiety and depression. This scare had come on the heels of a major surgery for me, as well as other stressors. In many ways, our son's diagnosis was simply the last straw. Through it all, I kept my depression very private. I sometimes had to crawl to the washroom in the morning because I had no strength to walk. Then I would pull myself together and continue on with the day.

In time I came to realize that I needed to see a doctor, and I was put on medication. Slowly the little cloud that hung over my eyes started to lift. God's hand on my life, time, my husband's love, and proper medical care all were part of those years. It took me years to realize that my depression was as physical as arthritis or cancer.

During those dark days, I would live for the nighttime, when I could sing in my head until sleep came. Night after night, I would repeat, "My Jesus, I love thee" or "Blessed Jesus, come to me."

All good things come from the Father above, and so it is to him I give credit for helping me through depression. I've come to realize that the helplessness I felt in my depression has led me to a greater dependence on God, who uses our trials to draw us into a closer relationship with him. I am so thankful that my joy does not depend on life's circumstances but rather on the One who came to this earth to give hope that the best is yet to come.

Lorella

PRAY

God, thank you for your promise that joy will eventually come. Be with all who struggle with depression and anxiety, and give us all a sense of your healing power.

SAVOR

What prayers or songs have helped you through seasons of anxiety or depression?

Week 5, Day 5
THORNS OR ROSES?

Count it all joy, my brothers, when you meet trials of various kinds,
for you know that the testing of your faith produces steadfastness.
And let steadfastness have its full effect, that you may be perfect and
complete, lacking in nothing. —JAMES 1:2-4 (ESV)

In our women's Bible study recently, we talked about suffering, trials, and persecution. We're studying Philippians, and "joy in everything" seems to be the theme of that book. So we discussed "joy in suffering." But what does that even mean?

My brother married my sister-in-law, Nina, knowing she had cystic fibrosis and that her life expectancy was short. Nina suffered for much of her adult life, struggling to breathe. After years of being in and out of the hospital, she had a double lung-heart transplant that improved her quality of life for a few years. She survived her illness longer than most and lived to thirty-six years of age.

Nina had joy in her suffering. I'll never forget her great attitude and the fun we had with her in the midst of her struggles. After her death, we found Bible verses that she had written in her journal, and we used them at her funeral. This was one of them: "So we do not lose heart. Though our outer self is wasting away, our inner self is being renewed day by day" (2 Corinthians 4:16 ESV).

The New Testament does not paint a rosy picture of the Christian life on this earth. Instead, it assures us that if we follow Christ, we will face trials and persecutions. Because we are identified with Christ, we will receive much of the same bad treatment and rejection he received.

Paul writes, "Indeed, all who desire to live a godly life in Christ Jesus will be persecuted" (2 Timothy 3:12 ESV). And Peter writes, "Beloved, do not be surprised at the fiery trial when it comes upon you to test you, as though something strange were happening to you" (1 Peter 4:12 ESV).

The thorny trials are inevitable. How will I react? How should I behave in the midst of these trials? Will I choose joy, trusting in almighty God and his plans and purposes? I hope so.

I want to experience steadfastness. I want to rejoice and be glad when Christ's glory is revealed. I choose to trust that God will teach me during my trials to react in a way that lets steadfastness have its full effect, bringing me homeward toward perfection and completeness.

I don't want a crown of roses now. I want a crown of life. That way, when I get to heaven, I can cast it at Jesus' feet.

Elle

PRAY

Jesus, give me joy in the middle of suffering. Help me remain steadfast.

SAVOR

Think about someone you've known who has been joyful in the middle of trials. How can you follow that person's example?

Week 5, Day 6

GOD'S LOVE LETTER

*I have stored up your word in my heart, that I
might not sin against you.* —PSALM 119:11 (ESV)

When our children went into the seventh grade, we gave each of
them a new Bible. Before we gave the Bible to them, however,
we invited our family members and friends to mark up the pages,
highlight verses, and write in the margins about why this or that verse
was important to them.

When our children started to read the Bible for themselves, these
verses would jump out at them. Knowing that certain Scriptures were
meaningful to the people in their lives made those Scriptures more
meaningful to them as well. It also encouraged our children to mark
up this sacred book and to make it more personal.

Reading the Bible is a very personal thing. We all have our own
way of reading it, the version we prefer, and the time of day we like to
sit back to read God's Word. Marking up the pages of a Bible can help
to make it even more meaningful.

When I was a young Christian, there were times that the Bible just
did not make any sense to me. I felt as though it was written in a way

that I just could not understand. Even when we don't understand all of it, however, the Bible is like a love letter from God—a guide to daily living, and a word of encouragement and hope. And who doesn't want to read a love letter?

My prayer is that you have a stirring within you to read God's Word, to mark up the book, and to make it personal. I pray that you too would learn for yourself that God loves you with an undying love, which he proved by giving us his Son, Jesus Christ.

PRAY

Lord, thank you for your love letter to humanity. Help me store up your Word in my heart.

SAVOR

When is your favorite time of day to read your Bible? How can you make your Bible reading more personal?

Week 5, Day 7

LOVE WORTH SAVORING

---

*Taste and see that the Lord is good; blessed is the
one who takes refuge in him.* —PSALM 34:8 (NIV)

As I wandered through my garden recently, I was drawn to the pot filled with different herbs that I use for cooking: oregano, mint, thyme, basil, and parsley. As I rubbed the herbs between my fingers, they released an aromatic fragrance, and I thought about how each herb adds the right flavor to the food I cook.

Each herb contributes its own distinctive flavor and brings out the best taste of the food. When I think of oregano, I think of the lovely flavor it adds to pizza sauce. Mint leaves bring wonderful flavored teas to mind, and just a sprig of mint can make a dish look so pretty. Parsley is an herb I use a lot in my kitchen. It adds a nice flavor to soups. Basil is a delight to add to tomato dishes.

This reminds me of God and of the richness I find in savoring and enjoying each morsel in his Word. These morsels speak to me of love, joy, hope, peace, and forgiveness. They are the "herbs of my soul," the qualities I want to cultivate and allow God to use to his glory. Some days my soul needs hope, on others I need to show forgiveness or extend love.

I am reminded not to rush as I read the Bible, but to let my mind absorb God's goodness and allow it to nourish my soul. When I read a verse of Scripture that speaks to me, I like to meditate on it throughout the day, seeing what Jesus is trying to teach me. Sometimes it's good to write out the verse and place it on my fridge or beside my computer, where I will see it often. Memorizing is another way to hide God's Word in my heart so that it will come to mind and comfort or encourage me when needed.

God's love is worth savoring.

PRAY
God, thank you for your goodness and your grace. Help me to savor your Word.

SAVOR
How do you "taste and see" the goodness of God throughout your day? What reminds you of God's love as you go through your daily routines?

WEEK 6

Family Journeys
FROM RUSSIA TO IRAN . . . ON FOOT

"Movement" was the theme of a sermon series at our church recently. As we launched into this series, our pastor encouraged us with this statement: "Acts tells the story of a group of first-century, ragtag followers of the risen Christ who became the movement that would change the world; it's God's movement because he is a God on the move, and he invites us to get on the move with him."

It's an encouraging exercise to look back over your life and the lives of your ancestors to see how God has led and moved you to where you are today.

Above: Ellen's parents (top row, second and third from left), with their families in a 1947 photograph taken in Iran. Ellen's mother holds her older sister, Kathy.

Part of my story is the fact that God moved both sets of my grandparents to flee Russia on foot with their children in the early 1930s. My grandparents all moved to Iran, settling near Tehran, where my parents later met and got married. Then God moved my father with the desire to come to the United States. One of the things that influenced this desire was how he was treated while working in a U.S. Army base kitchen in Iran. The soldiers were kind to my father and gave him food to take home to his family because they were struggling.

My parents filed the proper paperwork and were granted permission to immigrate to the United States. With my oldest sister they traveled to the United States, settling in Los Angeles shortly after World War II ended. In 1963 my father attended the Billy Graham crusades at the Los Angeles Memorial Coliseum and was born again.

My father's decision to follow Jesus turned my family's world upside down—in a good way. That same year I accepted Christ, and my new life in the greatest movement of all time began. We won't know the whole story of how our own lives influence God's movement until we see God face-to-face. But we can see part of the story now and be encouraged to carry on and follow him where he leads us. God doesn't call us and then leave us alone. He has given us his Spirit, who intercedes for us and gives us strength.

> *My father's decision to follow Jesus turned my family's world upside down—in a good way.*

When we are willing to step out in faith with him, God multiplies the little that we have. What an amazing movement to be a part of! You too can be a part of this movement. Ask God to reveal himself to you, to show you the way.

Ellen

Recipe

TANTE SUZIE'S BAKED BEANS

Serves 10

Advance preparation

- 4½ cups / 825 g dried navy beans
- 1 teaspoon / 5 ml baking soda
- 2 teaspoons / 10 ml salt

1. Soak beans in 12 cups / 3 L water overnight. Drain and rinse thoroughly.
2. Add 4 cups / 1 L fresh water, baking soda, and salt and simmer for 1 hour. Drain and rinse thoroughly.
3. Add beans to a bean pot (an oven-safe dish with lid will work), or use a slow cooker. Add the following ingredients.

Baked beans

- ½ pound / 225 g bacon, sliced
- ⅓ cup / 75 ml maple syrup
- ⅓ cup / 75 ml molasses
- 1 large onion, chopped
- 2 cloves garlic, minced
- 2 tablespoons / 30 ml brown sugar
- 2 teaspoons / 10 ml dry mustard
- 1 bay leaf
- 2 teaspoons / 10 ml salt
- 4 cups / 1 L tomato juice, plus additional as needed
- ½ pound / 225 g farmer sausage, cubed (optional)

1. Heat oven to 275° F / 135° C.
2. Disperse bacon evenly throughout the whole pot of beans.
3. In a bowl, combine syrup, molasses, onion, garlic, brown sugar, mustard, bay leaf, and salt, mixing thoroughly.
4. Pour mixture over beans and stir well.
5. Cover bean mixture with 4 cups / 1 L tomato juice.
6. Bake slowly, covered, for 5–6 hours, stirring hourly.
7. Add more tomato juice if the beans begin to get too dry.
8. If desired, add farmer sausage halfway through the cooking time.

I remember as a small girl attending the annual Schmidt gathering at Berthusen Park in Lynden, Washington. This bean pot, with its rich, smoked flavors, was always the signature dish brought by my *Tante* (aunt) Suzie. I was excited when my mother gave me a replica of this pot as a gift many years ago. Over the past years, families were busy, and we no longer gathered together. Just recently we have created a contemporary version of the Schmidt family reunion and have resurrected the original pot, which has given us many fond memories of good times together fifty years ago. "The trick to making beans," Tante Suzie would say, "is that they need to be baked in a bean pot." When the Schmidts get together today, we now share Tante Suzie's baked beans again.

Marg

GOD, RUNNING!

*So he got up and went to his father. But while he was still a long way
off, his father saw him and was filled with compassion for him; he ran to
his son, threw his arms around him and kissed him.* —**LUKE 15:20 (NIV)**

My father was big and strong, and often came across as being strict. Yet I have memories of the tenderness he showed when I was sick, the time he took for me when he was busy, and the hard-earned money he spent on me without complaining. His way of showing his love was in providing for us, guiding us, and protecting us.

As a grown woman now, I understand even more how my dad loved us. It is a natural feeling for a father to hope his children will recognize his love by what he has unselfishly given and done for them.

The most beautiful example of a father's love is described in the parable of the prodigal son. In this story, the son asks his father for his share of his forthcoming inheritance so he can go and spend it. I imagine the father would have loved to stop his son from making a huge mistake, but he let him go.

As the story goes, once the money is gone and the son is trying to stay alive by feeding pigs for a farmer, he comes to his senses and decides to go home. I love the description in Luke 15:20: "While he was still a long way off, his father saw him and was filled with compassion for him; he ran to his son, threw his arms around him and kissed him."

Can you imagine: God, running! The ultimate love of a father is depicted in teaching his children and watching them make choices that sadden him, yet waiting with open arms to forgive. Whether it's our natural father or our heavenly Father we envision in this scene, may we use this scene to reconcile the distance we may have created. Be assured that God's love is always waiting for us.

Anneliese

PRAY

Father God, thank you that you run toward me with such great and welcoming love.

SAVOR

Close your eyes and imagine your heavenly Father running toward you to embrace you. How might this image change your day?

Week 6, Day 2
PAY IT FORWARD

And do not forget to do good and to share with others, for with such sacrifices God is pleased. —HEBREWS 13:16 (NIV)

A few years ago I stood looking around a food court, trying to decide what to eat. As I debated the options and looked at the menu, a woman came up behind me and asked what I was having.

Thinking she was making conversation, I told her I thought I'd take number four on the menu. "Sounds good," she said, moving ahead of me in line. "I will get your lunch."

I sure was surprised when a stranger paid for my lunch that day. That incident has prompted me to "pay it forward": to show a caring and loving heart and to pass on the kindness to someone else.

I believe that God's plan for us includes paying it forward—selflessly giving to and doing for others—out of all we have received from him. I pray that our eyes will be open and that we will not miss opportunities to show God's love to others.

Imagine how different our world would be if we showed the kind of love that God has given us through his Son, Jesus! "Do not forget to do good and share with others," Hebrews 13:16 tells us. It's a small way to pay forward the love that Christ showed to us.

Little acts of kindness go a long way to encourage someone. Paying it forward can be as simple as making a phone call, sending a card in the mail, or giving flowers and a plate of cookies to someone going through a hard time. These little things mean so much.

Do one single act of kindness . . . and watch it multiply!

PRAY

God, you paid it forward for me; help me to pay it forward to others.

SAVOR

Have you ever had someone show you an unexpected act of kindness? What did it mean to you?

Week 6, Day 3
EVERLASTING ARMS

And in the wilderness, where you have seen how the Lord your God carried you, as a man carries his son. —DEUTERONOMY 1:31 (ESV)

On a recent Sunday, I sat in the pew behind a mother with her very small child. During the service, the child grew sleepy, and I watched him fall asleep in his mother's arms.

Nothing to me defines peace, contentment, and security as much as a baby asleep in his mother's arms. The world could be falling around him, but that baby has no fear, no worry. He is safe.

I thought of Jesus' disciples, who one day embarked on a journey across a lake but were caught in an angry storm. The wind lifted the water into high waves that crashed over the sides of their boat and threatened to sink it. The disciples, frantically bailing water, struggled to keep their craft afloat.

Where was Jesus? Right there in the boat with them. Was he helping them? No. He was fast asleep, enjoying the rocking motion of the sea. The disciples were astounded and asked him how he could sleep. Didn't he know they were sinking? Didn't he care that they were going to die?

But Jesus had no fear, no worry. He had been asleep in the arms of his Father. No harm could come to him. Shaking his head at his disciples' fear and doubt, Jesus merely spoke his Father's words to the storm, and it ceased.

If we see how perfectly trusting a child is when asleep in a parent's arms, how much more should we feel content when God says we are carried in his arms? I love what I read in Scripture about God's "father heart" toward his children.

The words of an old hymn say it so well: "What have I to dread / what have I to fear / leaning on the everlasting arms?"

Julie

PRAY

Father, thank you for carrying me in your arms. Help me to rest in you today.

SAVOR

Imagine yourself in the arms of God. How does it change your outlook today?

Week 6, Day 4
MANY WATERS
---

*Many waters cannot quench love; rivers cannot
sweep it away.* —SONG OF SONGS 8:7 (NIV)

My husband and I have visited Bridal Veil Falls many times throughout the years, as it's just a few minutes' drive from our doorstep. This is the sixth highest waterfall in Canada, with water tumbling almost four hundred feet over a smooth rock face and creating a bridal veil effect. Living nearby, we have also seen the devastation caused by those same waters during heavy rains.

I am reminded that "many waters cannot quench love," as the writer of Song of Songs says. Love is what keeps a marriage going. It gives comfort in the tough times, ignites laughter and joy, and provides refreshment.

Forty years ago we took our marriage vows before God and our family and friends. We were filled with hopes and dreams and never gave a thought to the "many waters" that would come our way. Oh, but they came: crop failures and financial worries in the early years, a serious car accident, death and disappointments within the family.

Though there have been many challenges and hardships along the way, there were none so great that they could sink our marriage. We were always aware that we were not on this journey alone, and that God was in control.

Jesus is the ultimate example of what love should look like. He loved even when he was rejected. He pursued us . . . found us . . . and gave his life for us. That is the kind of love with need in our marriages and families: love that will go to all lengths and that will prevail in good times and bad.

Through the good times and the bad, God has been there for us. We didn't wish to go through the rough waters, but our love and faith have been strengthened by those very things.

We know there are bound to be more rapids up ahead, and we plan to let God help us navigate them. Today we thank him for bringing us safely this far.

Judy

PRAY

Thank you, God, for your love that sustains us and protects us through many waters. Grant us that same kind of love for each other.

SAVOR

How have "many waters" strengthened your love for God? For your spouse or family?

Week 6, Day 5
EXPECTANT

---

*In the morning, Lord, you hear my voice; in the morning I lay my
requests before you and wait expectantly.* —PSALM 5:3 (NIV)

I am reading through Psalms, and I have noticed that the writer of
this book, David, is a man after God's own heart. David is a man
who cries out to God, prays to God, and praises him. David is able to
see the great miracles that God does despite all of David's sinful short-
comings and trials. David is so devoted to spending time with God
that he begins his day by listening for the voice of God. The psalmist
waits expectantly to hear from him.

That type of waiting is what I desire for myself. I don't want to just
pray and hope for the best. With a simple, trusting faith, I want to
wait expectantly for God to work things out in my life or in the lives
of the ones I love.

The one thing I have learned when I pray is that I will indeed have
to wait. Rarely does God's timing align with mine. The question is:
how will I wait? I can wait while doubting that God really cares and
hears my prayers. I can wonder what difference my prayers make

anyway. Or I can wait in hope, expecting and believing that God will answer with what is best for me or the situation—even if the answer is *not now* or *no*.

I want expectant waiting to become second nature for me. I want to seek God first thing in the morning every day, no matter what is happening in my life or how I feel at the time.

Are you going through a challenge in your life? Then take some time in the morning to bring your requests to God. Join me in waiting expectantly.

Week 6, Day 6

REIN THIS TONGUE

---

*If anyone thinks he is religious and does not bridle his tongue but
deceives his heart, this person's religion is worthless.* —**JAMES 1:26 (ESV)**

Are you thankful for your tongue? As someone who loves to cook
and bake, I rely on the taste buds on my tongue to tell me how
much seasoning and spice to add to my dishes. I feel quite confident in
the function of my taste buds.

The other function of my tongue has me less satisfied. On occasion
I have been reminded that bridling my tongue is still one of the most
challenging parts of my character development. In a conversation with
a friend, I blurted out a response to a hurtful comment. My feelings
of oversensitivity led to a response that was both unnecessary and
unkind. I was left feeling deep regret, and I had to take steps both to
forgive and to offer restitution.

Why do I still believe that my opinion needs to be broadcast? Why
do I still have such a hard time listening to others while they are speaking, thinking instead of how I will reply? Sometimes I get frustrated by
the small degree of control I seem to have on this part of my body.

In our church we have been doing a study in James. It didn't surprise me to find that this study is a rather uncomfortable one for me. It challenges me to be consistent in who I say I am, and it sometimes reveals to me the stark reality of how I behave.

If I don't rein in my tongue, my religion is worthless? Oh, Lord Jesus, I want to have a life that is honoring to you! I'm so thankful for forgiveness and for new beginnings. We can have confidence in God's forgiveness and grace when our tongues get the better of us.

Lovella

PRAY

With joy and thankfulness, I rejoice in you, Lord. Turn my tongue from things that displease you to things that honor and praise you.

SAVOR

When have you wanted to say something and then thought better of it? Count it a blessing from God!

Week 6, Day 7
GOD'S NEST

He who dwells in the shelter of the Most High will abide in the shadow of the Almighty. I will say to the Lord, "My refuge and my fortress, my God, in whom I trust." —**PSALM 91:1-2 (ESV)**

Our neighbor's house is sitting empty, waiting to be sold. On the front porch stands an artificial fig tree. This spring, it was considered prime real estate by two robins.

The tree was totally safe from predators, perfectly protected from the elements. The lawns close by offered an abundance of worms. Soon the mother robin laid her eggs in a neatly constructed nest, securely supported by the top branches.

I could not see into the nest because it was too high, so I decided to take a photograph to see the baby birds after they had hatched. I had to hold the camera up and snap the photo without looking through the viewfinder. I was so surprised to see the well-developed birds in my photo—and even more surprised that they sat perfectly still as I held the camera over them!

The next day I tried to take another picture, but this time the baby robins panicked and flew out of the nest—down across the lawn and between the houses. The parent birds were understandably upset. They called loudly for their young, who were now vulnerable. I hoped that these baby robins would stay safely on the ground until they were strong enough to fly with their parents.

Proverbs 27:8 says, "Like a bird that flees its nest is anyone who flees from his home" (NIV).

God has built us a nest that is perfectly safe from things that would harm us. His laws and commandments are designed to keep us impervious to the elements of this world. But how often we are like the young birds. How often the wisdom of this world seems wiser than the Word of God, and we yield to the enticing, flattering, or frightening voices around us.

Though we search the world over, we will find no place as lovely and secure as the secret place close to the heart of God.

Julie

WEEK 7

Family Journeys
WARM STONES FOR THE SLEIGH

In 1927 my father, Kornelius, a ten-year-old boy at the time, together with his parents and two siblings, emigrated from Ukraine to Canada on the ship *Montnairn*. What an adventure for a ten-year-old boy!

A number of years later, he met my mother, Maria, in a youth group that was often hosted by her parents. They got married in June 1939, and at first they lived in a little house in his parents' yard as they helped his father on the farm. Later he purchased his own farm, and this is where my memories began.

I can remember the times before we had electricity when my mother would help with the milking and farm chores. I was six years

Above: Betty's parents and their children in their horse-drawn sleigh. Betty is the baby in her mother's arms.

old and left to tend to my younger brother, who was still a baby and was often asleep in the crib. My mother would instruct me not to touch the kerosene lamp that sat in the middle of the table. She would come into the house frequently to check on us. My older brothers were helping in the barn at the time. She must have been in constant prayer for our well-being as she hurried through the chores.

During the first few years of my life, we did not own a car. In summer we would travel from place to place with a horse and buggy, and in winter we would travel with a horse and sleigh. I would sit at my mother's feet, leaning against the front end of the sleigh, facing her. Warm stones were placed by our feet, and we were bundled in blankets to stay warm.

She must have been in constant prayer for our well-being as she hurried through the chores.

Christmas was always a joyous and memorable time for us, because it meant extra treats. On Christmas Eve, before going to bed, we each put out an empty cookie sheet on the kitchen table. Once we were asleep, our parents would secretly decorate the Christmas tree and fill our cookie sheets with treats.

Early morning on Christmas Day, we would come bounding down the stairs and stand in awe of the beautiful tree. Then we would make a dash to the kitchen to see what Santa had left for us on our cookie sheets. Each cookie sheet would usually contain a mandarin orange, some candies, peanuts, and a coloring book and crayons that didn't need to be shared!

Once the farm chores were done, we would open our gifts. We each received one gift, which more than likely had been purchased at a thrift store. We did not mind that at all and felt very blessed!

A church from a local town came to our area to host a Sunday school class on Sunday afternoons. It was there that I first heard about

Jesus. My Sunday school teacher, Miss Martens, was instrumental in planting the seed that prompted me to ask Jesus into my heart. It was not until I was twenty-six years old that I made this decision to accept Christ into my heart.

In the winter of 1966, I met the love of my life, John. We married in the fall of 1967. We were blessed with three beautiful children—two daughters, Brenda and Alison, and a son, Jonathan. At the age of seven months, our son was diagnosed with tuberous sclerosis and later with autism. Many difficult years followed, and our faith was often tested. But we stayed the course. We knew that God had his hand in this situation, just as he had during the struggles that my parents and grandparents faced in immigrating to a new country and establishing a homestead.

Like a quilt-maker, God has pieced together my journey in life. God is still teaching me to depend on him in every circumstance.

Recipe

BAKED OATMEAL

Serves 6–8

- 2 eggs
- ½ cup / 125 ml brown sugar
- ¼ cup / 60 ml oil
- 3½ cups / 875 ml oats or quick oats (not instant)
- 2 teaspoons / 10 ml baking powder
- 1 teaspoon / 5 ml salt

- ½ teaspoon / 2 ml cinnamon
- ½ cup / 125 ml coconut or raisins (optional)
- 1 apple, grated (unpeeled if soft-skinned)
- 1 cup milk

1. With a wooden spoon, beat eggs and sugar well, then stir in oil.
2. Combine dry ingredients (oats, baking powder, salt, cinnamon, and coconut or raisins, if desired) and add to egg mixture.
3. Stir in the grated apple and milk.
4. Pour into a greased 8 x 8-inch / 20 x 20-cm pan or a large loaf pan.
5. Bake at 350° F / 175° C for about 30 minutes for square pan, or 40 minutes for loaf pan.
6. Serve warm with milk and sprinkle with toasted coconut or brown sugar, if desired.

This hearty, muffin-like version of breakfast oatmeal is delicious and easy to serve. You can prepare it the night before, refrigerate it, and bake it in the morning. I like to freeze a loaf, cut and wrapped in individual servings to warm up. These also make a good addition to packed lunches.

Anneliese

Week 7, Day 1
DRY GRASS

Consider how I love your precepts! Give me life according to your steadfast love. The sum of your word is truth, and every one of your righteous rules endures forever. —**PSALM 119:159-160 (ESV)**

We live on the beautiful coast of British Columbia. Locals are known to affectionately call our region the "Wet Coast." One recent summer, though, was unusually dry. Our farm took on a new look, with feathers from the chicken barns coordinating with the color of the dry grass.

Normally we mow the field every week in the summer to keep it tidy. But that summer the only things that needed mowing were the weeds! They still seemed to thrive.

As I walked across our dry field, I thought about our spiritual lives. When we don't do anything intentional to keep them nourished and thriving, our souls are a bit like a field during a drought. When we neglect worshiping with believers and reading the Bible, our struggles quickly become hard to overcome. We become dry and spent, as withered as brown grasses.

I also notice how encouraged I am when I am in church worshiping God, filling my soul with the truth of his lovingkindness for another week ahead. It's like receiving a beautiful rain. Worshiping God and reading Scripture helps to keep me green and pliable in the hands of God.

Let's encourage each other to keep our hearts and minds filled with the truths of God's Word. Those righteous truths nourish us and revive us.

Lovella

Week 7, Day 2
UNSHAKEN

Surely the righteous will never be shaken; they
will be remembered forever. —PSALM 112:6 (NIV)

My husband, Harv, and I were sitting at the kitchen table one
day in April, visiting with a friend, when Harv suddenly said,
"We're having an earthquake!"

My ever-observant husband had seen the light fixture begin to
sway. As we looked around, we saw the cords from the window blinds
swinging back and forth. Later, on the news, we received confirmation
that British Columbia had indeed been shaken. A 6.6-magnitude earthquake had been centered near Port Alice on Vancouver Island.

A phrase in Psalm 112:6 caught my attention later in the week.
What does it mean to be unshaken? It means standing firm when
everything around you is uncertain and giving way.

When others question your faith and their own, asking those really
hard questions, does your foundation remain firm? When illness
or death strikes, does it shake your trust in God's love and care?
When facing financial loss, when relationships crumble, where is

your foundation? These are questions that Psalm 112 brings to mind for me.

Psalm 18 declares, "The Lord is my rock, my fortress and my deliverer; my God is my rock, in whom I take refuge" (v. 2 NIV). And Psalm 62 affirms, "Truly he is my rock and my salvation; he is my fortress, I will never be shaken" (v. 2 NIV).

In this world there will be earthquakes. There will be times when we are fearful, times when we question God's presence in our lives, times when we call out in desperation as we feel the earth shake. However, the Bible assures us that God is our firm foundation, our solid rock. We can stand firm on him.

Bev

PRAY

God, you are our rock and fortress. When it feels as if everything is shaking around me, help me to find stability in you.

SAVOR

What do you think standing firm looks like? Is being "unshaken" the same as not being affected by life's difficulties?

Week 7, Day 3
FAITHFUL

The flowers appear on the earth, the time of singing has come, and the voice of the turtledove is heard in our land. —SONG OF SOLOMON 2:12 (ESV)

As I think about these words from the Song of Solomon, I have to wonder what wildflowers have to do with turtledoves. Then one word comes to mind: faithful.

Every spring, out of ground left dormant through a harsh winter, the flowers awaken out of a sweet sleep. Bright purple and yellow crocuses and white snowdrops burst forth, fresh and beautiful as they push up through the cold and frozen earth. And the turtledoves? The turtledoves, which mate for life, have become the emblem for love and faithfulness, inspiring poets and musicians alike.

What convincing evidence God has put into his creation to portray his faithfulness to us! His commitment to fulfill every promise he made to us can be counted on.

We take for granted that the wildflowers will bloom in the spring and that the turtledove will coo a love song to its mate. Just as surely as we can expect the flowers and the doves, we can trust in the God who is ever faithful to his promises. I hold onto these words of promise when situations or circumstances threaten to overwhelm me with discouragement or pain, when the heavens are overcast or the light of God's presence grows dim.

I think back to a time when, because of illness and loss of jobs, my husband and I did not know where our next meal was coming from, and there was no promise of a financial turnaround. My prayer through that testing time was "Lord, I know you are faithful and you have promised to supply our needs. I'm going to trust you." And God was faithful in ways that surprised and delighted us!

Julie

PRAY

God, thank you for your faithfulness. Give me trust in your steadfast faithfulness even when I can't see your work.

SAVOR

How did you experience God's faithfulness in the past week?

This is the day that the Lord has made; let us rejoice and be glad in it. —PSALM 118:24 (ESV)

During the last few weeks, I have had many conversations with people who admitted that they were waiting for something to change so that they could enjoy life more. These are some of the things I have heard:

"If only I had someone special to share my life with, then I would be . . ."

"If only I had that job I wanted, then I would be . . ."

"If only money weren't so tight, then I would be . . ."

"If only I had a bigger house, then I would be . . ."

"If only I could lose that last fifteen pounds, then I would be . . ."

I know that I've said things like this too. Does any of this sound familiar to you?

Psalm 118:24 is recited or sung so often. But do we even really think about what we are saying?

When I have read this verse before, what resonated with me was the part that says "let us rejoice and be glad in it." But recently, the two words that jump out at me are "This is."

I suffer from chronic pain due to an autoimmune arthritis. I often wish I was free of pain and able to enjoy doing the things that I once did with my family and friends. Yes, I get discouraged at times. But what I also know is that the Lord will turn every tear I have ever cried into joy. He knows everything about me, and he will use my pain for a greater purpose that he has planned for me. This is the day to rejoice—pain or no pain.

Are you waiting for something to change before you can say that Jesus is enough for you? I can't boast that I am there yet, but I am striving toward this kind of attitude.

So will you join me? This is the day. Today we will rejoice and be glad in it.

Charlotte

PRAY

Dear Jesus, help me to praise you this day. Thank you for being enough for me, right here and right now.

SAVOR

How can you rejoice in God this day? What can remind you of God's goodness today?

THE GOD WHO SEES

She gave this name to the Lord who spoke to her: "You are the God who sees me," for she said, "I have now seen the One who sees me."
—GENESIS 16:13 (NIV)

As a little girl, I felt uncomfortable with being told that God could see everything I did. It could be that this fact was portrayed in a negative manner. I remember one day taking a dark towel and covering up my window so that God wouldn't spy on me!

But I experience it differently now. Now I know that no matter what I've done, God sees me as one dearly loved. Being seen by God is an immense comfort and joy.

The Bible reminds us over and over again that God sees people—including those often overlooked by others—and that God's vision is filled with compassion and grace. We read the story of Hagar being mistreated and fleeing into the desert. When an angel speaks to her, Hagar calls out to God, saying, "You are the God who sees me."

The woman judged for "wasting perfume" on her Lord was honored by him. Jesus saw her heart, when other people only saw her sin.

The woman who gave her last penny was noted by Jesus as giving everything, when others snickered.

The woman at the well was offered water that would satisfy for life, even as she realized that Jesus knew everything about her search in all the wrong places.

The good news is that God sees and knows how we are made. God sees everything we are. Yet he loves us and calls us, just as we are. Knowing that God sees us confirms our importance to him.

Anneliese

PRAY

God, thank you for seeing me just as I am. Help me to see the world with your eyes.

SAVOR

How do you feel when you think about a God who sees you just as you are?

Week 7, Day 6

TEACH THEM TO YOUR CHILDREN

Impress them on your children. Talk about them when you sit at home and when you walk along the road, when you lie down and when you get up. Tie them as symbols on your hands and bind them on your foreheads. Write them on the doorframes of your houses and on your gates. —DEUTERONOMY 6:7-9 (NIV)

When I was a young parent, I remembered hearing these words from Deuteronomy. They have been embedded in my heart for years and years. I love visual learning, and this commandment could not have been better said for a visual learner. What would it look like if I went running around with ribbons tied on my fingers? What if I posted verses all over the doors and windows? Can you imagine what people would be thinking of me?

This Scripture reminds us of the influence parents have on their children's spiritual growth. We teach our children during the daily tasks and events of life, whether we know it or not. It's impossible to save the whole world, but the impact of living a godly life and parenting in a godly way will leave behind a ripple effect that reaches the lives of our children. This is our responsibility. If we don't teach our children to follow Christ, the world will teach them not to.

This past year I have had the pleasure of working through *One Thousand Gifts* by Ann Voskamp. She illustrates how we can stop and marvel at the depth and detail, the light and shadow, of all the scattered moments in life. In our day-to-day living, whether cleaning up children's rooms or washing their clothes or baking them cookies, we can pray and give thanks for the next generation.

Today, my heart warms as I think of parents teaching young children to bow down quietly in reverence before their Maker. Let's encourage one another in teaching our children and grandchildren the truths. Words from Scripture are precious gifts to the next generation; in passing them on, we hand on the legacy of faith.

Whether we are young or old, we can remind ourselves and others to see the daily blessings that God gives to us. Maybe we won't literally tie verses to our foreheads, but let's encourage each other and our children to remember the sweet words of Scripture—and to live them out.

Marg

Week 7, Day 7
TAKE A SNOW DAY

Jesus, full of the Holy Spirit, left the Jordan and was led by the Spirit into the wilderness. —LUKE 4:1 (NIV)

I have fond memories of one particular winter day when my family was snowed in. There were no errands to run, no need to bundle the kids for school. No one could go to work, and for a day I felt complete calm. My family was together, and there were no outside influences grabbing our attention away from home and each other.

Do you ever feel that the world and its demands—rushing here, there, striving for bigger, better, more beautiful, more stuff—has left you feeling lonely and empty? Grown children have little time for their aging parents. Parents are so busy trying to make a living for their family that parents actually don't have time for their children. They think they have to give their kids opportunities and stuff. Children's lives are often so overscheduled that they show signs of stress at younger and younger ages.

"Everybody today seems to be in such a terrible rush, anxious for greater developments and greater riches and so on," Mother Teresa once said. "Parents have very little time for each other, and in the home begins the disruption of peace in the world."

I would invite you to find a day—perhaps even today—to just slooow down. Stop. Reflect. Give yourself a snow day! You can do this even if it's not winter. If you have a family living at home, play a game or build an indoor or outdoor fort. If you have a friend you haven't talked to in a long time, give her a call and let her know that you are thinking of her. If you need a day for yourself to retreat, reflect, and rest, take your Bible and a journal to a favorite spot and don't answer your phone or check email.

Even Jesus had times in his life when he needed a "snow day"— that is, time apart to pray and get closer to God. Even Jesus needed time apart from his normal routine to reflect on God's love, grace, and mercy in his life.

Shouldn't we do the same? Go ahead: take a snow day!

Charlotte

PRAY

Jesus, thank you for modeling for us time apart from schedules and routines. Help me to find time to rest in your love and mercy.

SAVOR

How can you take a "snow day" sometime in the next few weeks?

WEEK 8

 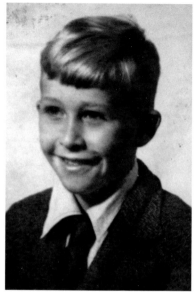

Family Journeys
AN (EXTRA)ORDINARY LOVE STORY

On a cold winter day in 1937, a young couple in Gnadenfeldt, Ukraine, welcomed the birth of their first child, a son. Their expectation that life would continue in pleasant ways was not to be. How fearfully they would have looked into the future if they could have seen what was coming.

For a short few years, all was well. But then life began to change. The father was marched off to Siberia with the other men of the village. The little boy never saw him again. His mother, now left with three little boys, one a baby, was forced to flee with the other village women and children and the few remaining men. They used the

Above, left: Julie, nine months old, in 1948. Above, right: Vic, eleven years old, soon after he arrived in Canada in 1948.

retreating German army as their rear guard. The trek was terror-filled, with narrow escapes from death and injury. They were robbed of home, family, and everything familiar, and they were left facing the unknown of what life would be. Traveling by horse and buggy, with the few possessions they could take with them, they fled the Ukraine through Poland and into Germany.

Finally, they found a safe haven in the Netherlands for two years, until, sponsored by the mother's brother, they immigrated to Canada in the spring of 1948.

Meanwhile . . .

On a hot summer day in 1947, a young couple in Chilliwack, British Columbia, welcomed the birth of their first child, a daughter. The war was over, and the future looked promising. When their baby was three months old, the parents moved to Abbotsford, to a hobby farm where the girl and her siblings were happily raised, free from the fear of war and uncertainty. They made West Abbotsford Mennonite Church their home church.

As I look back over my life, I am astounded at the way the Lord has led me—often when I was not aware of it.

It was the same church the boy attended when his mother also made their home in Abbotsford. The boy watched the little girl grow up, and one day, on a hike with the young people from their church, he singled her out. Both felt something special sparked between them that day, and after dating for two years, they got married. They had a daughter, they gained a son-in-law, and they were blessed with two beautiful granddaughters. They recently celebrated fifty years of marriage.

The boy is my husband, Vic. The girl is me.

As I look back over my life, I am more and more astounded at the way the Lord has led me—often when I was not at all aware of it. Situations, events, and circumstances that I would have dismissed and forgotten about were actually ways that God's hand was weaving my life according to his purposes. In many ways, I would describe my life as an ordinary one. But on another level I have to describe it as extraordinary—with the *extra* all because of God.

A passage of Scripture that I hold as my life motto comes from Jeremiah: "Thus says the Lord: 'Let not the wise man boast in his wisdom, let not the mighty man boast in his might, let not the rich man boast in his riches, but let him who boasts boast in this, that he understands and knows me" (Jeremiah 9:23-24 ESV).

Nothing in life has meaning, nothing in life is satisfying, nothing in life brings peace or joy . . . except knowing and understanding God. I can trust completely in his love to wisely guide me through all the days of my earthly sojourn.

Julie

Recipe
CREAMY RICE PUDDING

Serves 4–6

- 4 cups / 1 L milk
- ½ cup / 125 ml short-grain rice
- ⅛ teaspoon / 0.5 ml salt
- ¼ cup / 60 ml raisins (optional)

- 1 egg
- ⅓ cup / 75 ml sugar
- 1 teaspoon / 5 ml vanilla extract
- Cinnamon (optional)

1. Heat milk, rice, and salt on medium heat. (Using medium heat is very important; otherwise you will scorch the milk and burn the pudding.)
2. Bring to a boil, stirring almost constantly. Be patient, as this takes a few minutes.
3. Reduce the heat and simmer for 30 minutes. Add raisins at this time, if desired.
4. In a separate bowl, mix the egg, sugar, and vanilla.
5. Take about half the cooked rice and slowly whisk it into the egg mixture.
6. Stir the rice-egg mixture into the remaining rice and continue to cook on low heat for 2–3 minutes.
7. Serve warm or cooled completely. If you are cooling it completely, cover the pudding with plastic wrap so it will not form a skin. Individuals may wish to top their servings with cinnamon if desired.

When I was growing up, rice cooked in milk and sprinkled with sugar and cinnamon was one of my favorite things. I have been making this simple dessert for years now. With the increasing number of people on gluten-free diets, this is a good alternative to serve as a dessert. It also works well if you use coconut milk as a dairy substitute. This pudding has a delicate, creamy texture and is not too sweet. Make sure you prepare enough, because the bowl gets licked clean!

Charlotte

Week 8, Day 1
WHEREVER YOU GO

Have I not commanded you? Be strong and courageous. Do not be frightened, and do not be dismayed, for the Lord your God is with you wherever you go. —JOSHUA 1:9 (ESV)

At seven months old, our son was diagnosed with tuberous sclerosis. Later he was diagnosed with autism as well. John and I were not given much hope that he would ever walk, speak, or function normally. We were told that we would have to deal with seizures, mood swings, anger, and other behavioral problems.

When our son was diagnosed, we clung to verses like this one from Joshua to help us through the hard times. Our son is now forty years old, and there have indeed been many challenges and rough patches in the journey. We still have to go through the hard times. But God is with us, giving us the courage and strength that we need.

This verse is an encouragement for all of us, especially when we feel weak and discouraged. It is a promise to us that we are never alone. God commanded Joshua to be strong and courageous as he led the Hebrew people across the Jordan. We can be strong and filled with courage, because we know that God is with us at all times and through every trial we face.

When we feel discouraged, weak, or afraid, we can diligently search God's Word. In verse after verse, in the Old Testament and the New, we discover that God wants to give us strength and peace for the circumstances in which we find ourselves. Wherever we go, God goes with us.

Week 8, Day 2
FAMILY PARTY

So then you are no longer strangers and aliens, but you are fellow citizens with the saints and members of the household of God.
—EPHESIANS 2:19 (ESV)

A recent month was all about family. It started with a family reunion in Ontario, when my mom's siblings and their families gathered. It was wonderful time of renewing family relationships that had been restricted because of time and distance. There was joy in welcoming the newest members and a sense of loss over those who had passed on.

When we got home, our daughter and grandsons came for a visit. Because they live several provinces away, we don't see them often, so a visit is a time to check on how much the boys have grown, make opportunities for the cousins to play, and find fun things for the family to do together.

One of the reasons for their visit was the marriage of our nephew. Two who are dear to us had fallen in love and were making a commitment to become one. We joyously celebrated the occasion of their marriage.

At the end of the month, my husband and I invited friends and family to join us as we celebrated our fortieth wedding anniversary. Like every husband and wife, we've had good times and difficult ones, but our love for each other has carried us through to this day, and so we celebrate.

In the Christian life, we also celebrate family. When someone is born into the family of God, the Bible tells us that all heaven rejoices. When a member of God's family goes through difficulties, we do our best to support them through prayer and practical help.

We are saddened when one of God's children chooses to leave the family, and we rejoice when the family relationship is restored.

Finally, there is the promise of a wonderful family reunion to look forward to. When Christ returns, he will gather the whole family of God together, and the celebration will be never-ending.

What a family party that will be!

Bev

PRAY

God, thank you for the incredible privilege of being part of your family. Help me to invite others to join.

SAVOR

How can you celebrate being part of the family of God?

Week 8, Day 3
SCARS FOR SWEETNESS

Blessed be the God and Father of our Lord Jesus Christ, the Father of mercies and God of all comfort, who comforts us in all our affliction, so that we may be able to comfort those who are in any affliction, with the comfort with which we ourselves are comforted by God. —2 CORINTHIANS 1:3-4 (ESV)

It was cherry season, and at our Bible study group we were served a bowl of fresh cherries.

Rick, our friend and host, shared an interesting insight that he had regarding cherries. He told how he used to examine them and would set aside any cherry that was not "perfect." Then one day he discovered that the ones with scars or blemishes were sweeter than those without flaws. He commented how he hoped that though he was scarred by sin and failure, God would still find some sweetness in him as well.

Curious, I did some online research when I got home and found that Rick was right. Cherries with scars are indeed sweeter. One cause of a cherry's blemish is when the fruit rubs against a branch as it is forming and ripening.

What a beautiful spiritual analogy is portrayed here! All of us can point to personal scars or imperfections. We are flawed by rubbing against the unavoidable, painful, and difficult circumstances of life.

In response, it is easy to put up walls of self-defense. We tend to concentrate on the "scar" rather than acknowledge that the challenges of life build character, give us strength, and cause us to become who God intends us to be. The scars are simply the evidence that we have been tried and tested.

The question then becomes: Are we sweeter for it? Scripture tells us that we can only comfort others with the comfort that we ourselves have experienced in our times of need or suffering. Our difficulties teach us the wisdom we need to minister to others in the sweetness of love and compassion.

Julie

PRAY

God, help me to see my scars as beautiful rather than shameful. Help me to comfort others out of the great comfort I have received from you.

SAVOR

What "branches" have marred your spirit? How do those scars help you minister to and comfort others?

Week 8, Day 4
WHATEVER

So Jesus answered and said to them, "Assuredly, I say to you, if you
have faith and do not doubt, you will not only do what was done to
the fig tree, but also if you say to this mountain, 'Be removed and
be cast into the sea,' it will be done. And whatever things you ask in
*prayer, believing, you will receive." —*MATTHEW 21:21-22 (NKJV)

It came as a wee insert in a birthday card some weeks ago: a little card that said in big letters, "Whatever!" Underneath, it said, "And whatever things you ask in prayer, believing, you will receive."

Whatever: that word caught my eye. It is often used to end a discussion. Sometimes it expresses exasperation. At times it comes as a parting shot at the end of a conversation.

But maybe we need to rethink that word. It is a powerful word, and in the Bible, it appears often. It means something like "no matter what" or "regardless of the circumstance."

The apostle Paul used it frequently. He writes in Philippians, "Finally, brothers, whatever is true, whatever is honorable, whatever is just, whatever is pure, whatever is lovely, whatever is commendable, if there is any excellence, if there is anything worthy of praise, think about these things" (Philippians 4:8 ESV). Elsewhere Paul writes, "For I have learned in whatever situation I am to be content"; "Whatever you do, do all to the glory of God"; "Whatever one sows, that will he also reap"; and "Whatever good anyone does, this he will receive back from the Lord" (Philippians 4:11 ESV; 1 Corinthians 10:31 ESV; Galatians 6:7 ESV; Ephesians 6:8 ESV).

And then there is my favorite—the verse on the little card that I've now posted in my office. "And whatever things you ask in prayer, believing, you will receive" (Matthew 21:22 NKJV).

Despite the way it's often used, in exasperation and accompanied by rolling eyes, we would do well to reclaim the word *whatever*. God helps us be faithful whatever we face. God helps us choose to follow him whatever the circumstance. Whatever happens, we know God is with us.

Judy

PRAY

God, help me to be faithful whatever happens.

SAVOR

Choose one of the passages mentioned above and meditate on it. How can you stay faithful to the instruction of the verse, no matter what happens today?

Week 8, Day 5

BREAD OF LIFE

Your word is a lamp for my feet, a light
on my path. —**PSALM 119:105 (NIV)**

During a recent year, the ten ladies of Mennonite Girls Can Cook nudged each other to spend more time in God's Word. Through email we began to share what we were reading in our personal devotions, as well as praise and prayer items. We eventually chose Wednesday as our day to specifically share a verse that has been meaningful to us during the week. What an encouragement this has been!

Spending time reading the Bible takes discipline. I spend far more time in prayer than I do in reading my Bible. I can pray anywhere and at any time—what a blessing that is! Bible reading, on the other hand, requires me to stop. It requires time. Stopping and finding time? Those things take discipline.

God's Word is the bread of life. We can never overindulge in it. It is soul food that I need every day. At times I have starved myself, not getting enough. Then, after seasons when I haven't read the Bible very much, I've sometimes reached a point of craving it.

When I discipline myself to stop and take time to read Scripture, I am fed well. God's Word is spiritually healthy nourishment. God's Word is fresh. At times it is a feast for my soul, a feast in which my deepest spiritual hunger is nourished. At other times, it is a small bite that refreshes for the moment.

A lamp, a light, a loaf of bread: all of these images for Scripture demonstrate how important it is to our lives. We can't live without light, and we can't live without food.

Kathy

PRAY

God, thank you for giving me nourishment through your Word. Help me to find time and to make space for reading it so that I can encounter you in its pages.

SAVOR

How has Scripture fed your soul?

Week 8, Day 6
FRESH EYES

*Make a joyful noise to the Lord, all the earth! Serve the Lord with
gladness! Come into his presence with singing!* —PSALM 100:1-2 (ESV)

Last Saturday I visited a beautiful woodland garden that is only
open to the public a few times a year. I was struck by all the vari-
eties of plants that the gardener had grown and the labor it takes to
create the beautiful spaces that I was able to walk through. This garden featured trilliums, which are endangered wildflowers that appear
in the woods in the springtime. Their native habitats are shrinking
and they are becoming rarer and hard to find. Trilliums are known for
having three flower petals and three leaves, and come in many colors,
including white, yellow, pink, red, brown, and green.

My time in that garden reminded me of our own Master Gardener,
who has created all these things for us to enjoy. Psalm 100 invites the
earth itself to make a joyful noise in praise of God.

If you need a reminder of God's goodness to us, step out into the
world that he has created. Visit a garden or a meadow, or just take a
walk around your neighborhood. What sounds do you hear? What

new growth catches your eye? Open your eyes to see something new that you haven't noticed before.

Sometimes we forget to look around at the gifts of God that are right before us. We take for granted the beauty that surrounds us. Ask God to open your eyes to see, and you will have cause to worship God again with fresh eyes.

Ellen

Week 8, Day 7

A LINK IN THE CHAIN

Love is patient and kind; love does not envy or boast; it is not arrogant or rude. It does not insist on its own way; it is not irritable or resentful; it does not rejoice at wrongdoing, but rejoices with the truth. Love bears all things, believes all things, hopes all things, endures all things. —1 CORINTHIANS 13:4-7 (ESV)

Dietrich Bonhoeffer was a German Lutheran pastor of extraordinary conscience. Put into a Nazi concentration camp during World War II for his strong opposition to Hitler, Bonhoeffer was executed shortly before Germany surrendered in 1945.

Many people know of Bonhoeffer's writings on following Jesus and resisting evil, but few know about his writings on marriage. During his time in prison, Bonhoeffer's niece got married. Had he not been imprisoned, Bonhoeffer would have certainly officiated at her wedding ceremony.

Bonhoeffer decided to write a sermon, which was smuggled out of prison and read out loud at her wedding. "Marriage is more than your love for each other," Bonhoeffer wrote to his niece and her new husband.

In your love you see only your two selves in the world, but in marriage you are a link in the chain of generations. . . . In your love you see only the heaven of your own happiness, but in marriage you are placed at a post of responsibility toward the world and mankind. Your love is your own private possession, but marriage is more than something personal—it is a status, an office.

If you are in the planning stages of your marriage, seek a godly marriage course that will get you off to the best possible start. Speaking from experience, I can say that seeing your marriage as a "position of responsibility" and a link between generations will help you stay true when the going gets tough. Ask God to help you make your marriage into a blessing to others, not just to yourselves.

Lorella

PRAY

God, thank you for the gift of marriage and for the blessings of faithful marriage throughout generations.

SAVOR

If you are married, how can you make your marriage more than a private, personal thing? If you aren't married, what can you do to support the marriages of others?

WEEK 9

Family Journeys
SAFE SPOT FOR THE SOUL

During a recent summer, I took some time to reflect on my grand-father's memoirs. He was born in 1897 in the Ukraine, in the village of Steinfeld. He recalls how his father, my great-grandfather, taught him at a very early age to pray and sing songs to the Lord. My great-grandfather prioritized singing with his children and telling them wonderful Bible stories. His love for education and music gave him the ability to teach people how to sing four-part harmony. This method of singing soon spread to other villages and became a blessing to all. My grandfather's love of music, learned from his own father, is a legacy in my life.

Above: Marg's grandfather taught people to sing hymns such as this one, "Großer Gott, wir loben dich" ("Holy God, We Praise Thy Name"), in four-part harmony. This song remains a favorite hymn of worship for many who grew up in German-speaking churches.

Music has always been a large part of my life. I've experienced it as a language that has an extraordinary power to speak to my heart. I can remember going to my grandmother's house at a very early age and sitting down to play the piano. It did not take me long to learn to play "Jesus Loves Me."

I also remember standing at the kitchen sink, singing hymns with my mother as we did the dishes. I was fascinated with how our voices harmonized. What was it about this harmony that captivated me at such an early age? Perhaps this was a bonding with my mother and me, and a time I felt our hearts were knit together. It was a safe spot in my soul. Maybe that's what Grandpa was referring to when he remembers singing at an early age.

When I was twelve years old, my parents purchased our first piano. I've always been drawn to classical music, and I proceeded quickly through the Conservatory of Music program. Having enjoyed a rich musical upbringing, I participated in countless choirs in school, church, and college. Singing Handel's *Messiah* and Haydn's *Creation* has been a highlight in my life. These two outstanding oratorios speak of God's creation story and of Jesus' birth, crucifixion, and resurrection. I discovered that music is a way of feeding my spirit and that it allows me to respond to God.

> *I remember standing at the kitchen sink, singing hymns with my mother as we did the dishes. What was it about this harmony that captivated me?*

On our wedding day, my husband, John, presented me with an exceptional gift, which was an expression of deep love from his heart: a piano. It brings me joy to sit down and let my fingers flow over the keyboard, playing a variety of music, from hymns to the classics.

Music keeps drawing me back to God, from whom I get my strength. The song "Faithful One" by Brian Doerksen gave me inner strength and courage during a challenging season in my life. I'm wondering which timeless hymn my grandfather would have chosen during the difficult periods of his life.

This past Christmas, I had the opportunity to sing in a Handel sing-along performance in my own community. Tears streamed down my face as I was moved with joy in response to the musical harmonies and as I reflected on my grandfather's ability to sing "Glory to God."

In our home, our morning routine is to turn on music; it's just as important as that first cup of fresh coffee. Today I joyfully watch my grandchildren sit down at my piano and finger their own musical melodies. The legacy passed down from my grandfather to me continues to flow from me to my children and grandchildren.

Recipe
SALT AND PEPPER WINGS

Yields 24–30 prepared wings

- 3 pounds / 1.3 kg chicken wings
- 3 tablespoons / 45 ml soy sauce
- Kosher salt, to taste
- Montreal steak spice, to taste
- Lemon pepper, to taste
- Coarsely ground black pepper, to taste

1. Line a rimmed baking sheet with heavy-duty tinfoil and place a wire rack in the pan.
2. Cut each wing into 3 pieces. Discard wing tips or save for making soup.
3. In a large bowl, toss chicken wings with soy sauce until well coated.
4. Lay wings on rack so that they do not touch each other.
5. Sprinkle with seasonings.

6. Place in oven preheated to 400° F / 205° C and bake for
   30 minutes.
7. Remove from oven, turn each wing over, and bake for another
   20–30 minutes.

These wings are a hit each time I make them. A bonus is that they
have far fewer calories than many other recipes for chicken wings.

TIPS

*Use a sparing amount of kosher salt, as the soy sauce is already salty
and the steak spice usually has salt in it as well. The amount of Montreal steak spice, lemon pepper, and black pepper will depend on your
household's tastes.*

*These can be made a day or two ahead and refrigerated until needed.
Reheat them for 10–15 minutes at 400° F / 205° C.*

Bev

Week 9, Day 1
CHOOSE THIS DAY

Choose for yourselves this day whom you will serve. . . . But as for me and my household, we will serve the Lord. —JOSHUA 24:15 (NIV)

My husband, Harv, and I chose this verse for our wedding many years ago. We were very young and had little experience. But we did have examples in our parents and grandparents, who chose to serve God through good and bad. When pledging our marriage vows, we consciously chose to make God the foundation of our marriage—and our lives—each and every day.

With all the wars, famine, tsunamis, earthquakes, and refugee crises, one may be tempted to ask, "Is there really a God? If there is, why is this world in such a mess?" We read verses about God answering prayers, and yet at times our prayers don't seem to have much effect. We are told in the Bible that God heals, but we still suffer and die from illnesses. We read that God will never abandon the righteous, and yet some face trial after trial.

Maybe you have had questions about your faith, as I have. Is there a way to know, absolutely and without a doubt, that God exists? That God is loving? How can we know?

My conclusion is that we can't. We can't prove anything. But each day we can choose to believe in God, and in his love for us. Each day we can choose to believe in his righteousness, his holiness, and his promises of eternal life.

This is where faith comes in: believing in that which we cannot see or verify as fact.

And I do choose to believe . . . I choose this day whom to believe in and whom to serve.

God is my rock and my salvation, and I will follow him.

Yesterday's choice to serve the Lord isn't good enough for today. Just as Joshua did on that day so long ago, we too can choose this day whom we will serve.

Bev

PRAY

Lord, help me to believe in you and serve you anew each day. Today I choose you above all else.

SAVOR

In what small way can you choose to serve the Lord today?

LOVE: THE GREATEST AIM

*Let love be your greatest aim; nevertheless, ask also for the special abili-
ties the Holy Spirit gives, and especially the gift of prophecy, being able
to preach the messages of God.* —1 CORINTHIANS 14:1 (THE LIVING BIBLE)

Forty years ago I walked down the wedding aisle to be married to
the man of my dreams. The theme for our wedding was "Let Love
Be Your Greatest Aim" from 1 Corinthians 14:1.

I am awed as I sit here and reflect on God's graciousness to us
during the past forty years. Marriage for forty years. What does it
mean? What have we learned?

Here are a few golden nuggets that have shaped our lives over the
past years as "lifemates." May they guide and help you as well.

Whose marriage inspires you? Hang out with them.

Many times we dwell on problems but do not take the time to look
at solutions. Focus on growth. This does not happen overnight; it
takes determination and energy.

Did God design marriage to make us happy? I believe he wants us
to be happy, but more than that, he wants us to become holy.

Romance is wonderful, but it has no elasticity. It cannot be stretched. You can't depend on romance to get you through your life. Mature love built on the foundation of God, on the other hand, can stretch and last.

Challenges in marriage have given us opportunities to learn more about spiritual advancement.

Marriage forces us to face some character issues we'd never face otherwise.

Respect each other, allowing God to call each one to recognize what is highly important.

Know what you can expect from each other, and don't make unrealistic expectations.

Discover and share the same core values. For us, those values include family, faith, friends, and food.

When things don't work out as planned, be willing to compromise and let God redirect and reshape your dreams.

Learn to be intentional in your marriage and to enjoy and savor each day.

Make love your greatest aim.

Marg

PRAY
God, thank you for the gift of marriage. Make love our greatest aim.

SAVOR
How can you make love your greatest aim today?

Week 9, Day 3
RULES TO LIVE BY

*I can do all this through him who gives
me strength.* —**PHILIPPIANS 4:13 (NIV)**

Ever since I can remember, my dad has been a person of encouragement and one who speaks the truth. Many years ago he made a list for himself that he titled "Rules to Live By." At appropriate times in our adult lives, Dad has shared his personal life rules with us as a means of encouragement.

Attached to each of his short and direct rules is the key to what keeps this list from being legalistic: Scripture. Scripture is not a list of rules, but rather truth, spoken by God. Scripture is filled with guidance and encouragement to live by—all spoken out of God's great love for us.

When I read my dad's list of rules, my first thought is usually "Really? I can't follow these!" Then I go to Scripture, to Philippians 4:13, and God says to me, "Yes, you can do all things with my help."

I share with you my dad's list, in the hope that it will strengthen your day:

1. Never complain: "Rejoice always: pray continually; give thanks in all circumstances, for this is God's will for you in Christ Jesus" (1 Thessalonians 5:16-18 NIV).
2. Never give up: "Be strong and very courageous" (Joshua 1:7a NIV).
3. Never feel sorry for yourself: "So we make it our goal to please him" (2 Corinthians 5:9a NIV).

Do you have people who speak encouragement and truth into your life? Are you listening to the encouragements and truths from God as you read his Word?

Kathy

PRAY

God, give me strength to live out what I read in your Word.

SAVOR

Choose one of these rules to live by. How could you live it out today?

Week 9, Day 4

SEASONS OF CHANGE

*There is a time for everything, and a season for every
activity under the heavens.* —ECCLESIASTES 3:1 (NIV)

The seasons have just changed again, and I have loved watching my red sunset maple tree turn color. Have you ever noticed that leaves are most beautiful just before they drop? Those bright red, crimson colors are so stunning. And before you know it, they are gone.

For a long time, I seemed to be in the spring season of my life: newborns, growing families, financial decisions for supporting education and careers. And soon it became summer: the season to rest a bit, as now the children were making their own decisions and reaching their own accomplishments. They became independent, found their marriage partners and vocations, and one by one left home.

I just need to look at my hands to know what season of life I am now in: autumn. In this season I have time to reflect and gain new perspective. It's fun to think of memories, to make photo albums, and to stroll through the back roads of my mind. It's during this season that the foliage changes, the weather changes, and so does the time. Reflecting on the years gone by and watching the grandchildren grow brings new life again.

I want to be known as someone who can bring about beauty and strength. In every change, in every falling leaf, there is some pain, some beauty. And that's the way new leaves grow. We too can leave a legacy of beauty. During our autumn season, we still have time to encourage and influence those around us. We still have freedom to make choices and decisions. We can still gently guide our grandchildren, as we know they are fragile, and we have a chance to handle them with care. We can become their spiritual rocks during the hard times.

God has appointed the times and seasons, the events of our lives, the happy and the sad, the easy and the difficult. Let's make the best of each season and every day. We know that God will never change his mind about us.

PRAY

God, I turn the seasons of my life over to you. Help me accept the changing of life's seasons with grace and peace.

SAVOR

What season of life are you in? How can you turn toward God in this season?

Week 9, Day 5
ENSNARED

For freedom Christ has set us free; stand firm therefore, and do not submit again to a yoke of slavery. —**GALATIANS 5:1 (ESV)**

My daughter has a bird feeder in her backyard, but of course the birds are not the only ones to have found this delectable food source. The squirrels are regulars at this feeding station. But the other day a squirrel's greed almost cost him his life.

Just before my daughter and her family left the house, my daughter saw him hanging upside down on the feeder, gorging his cheeks full of birdseed. They returned four hours later, and he was still in the same position, filling his cheeks and body with the seed.

Something seemed amiss. Upon inspection, they realized that the squirrel, in securing his position, had wrapped his tail around the coiled wire elbow in the post from which the feeder hung. When he wanted to let go, his furry tail got tangled in the coil. In trying to get loose, he simply twisted his tail a few more times.

Undaunted by his inability to get free, he continued to eat. My son-in-law finally went out with wire cutters to cut the coil, setting the squirrel free (minus some fur and the tip of his tail). I'm sure he went home with an upset stomach and an aching tail!

Are we not just like that squirrel? We are entangled in Satan's snare, our eternity in question, yet we gorge ourselves with the goodies this world offers. We might make a bit of an effort to free ourselves, but we continue to consume the things our greed tempts us with.

Just as my son-in-law freed the squirrel who could not free himself, so also God sent Jesus to cut us free from the bondage of sin that entangles us. Jesus has provided the "wire cutters" of the cross. We need only to accept what Jesus has done for us. Then we can enjoy the freedom for which God created us!

Julie

PRAY

God, thank you for freeing me from sin that entangles. Help me to accept your good gift of freedom.

SAVOR

What has been ensnaring you recently? How can Jesus set you free from it?

Week 9, Day 6

FORGIVENESS AND FLOWERS

If we confess our sins, he is faithful and just to forgive us our sins and to cleanse us from all unrighteousness. —1 JOHN 1:9 (ESV)

I love how sunflowers always turn their faces toward the sun to bask in the fullness of its goodness. They're so graceful. It's as if they trust the sun fully.

I like to think that I turn my face toward God in the same way, but often something keeps my head bent in the other direction. I often find myself in a place where I need to seek forgiveness from someone I have hurt or wronged. Sometimes I need to forgive someone else who has, knowingly or unknowingly, hurt me. Somehow I find it easier to forgive someone else than to ask forgiveness. Sometimes the most difficult thing is to forgive myself!

Do you have difficulty forgiving yourself for mistakes you have made in your life? Perhaps you said something that should have been left unsaid. Maybe it was a poor choice you made a long time ago that you cannot go back and correct. Perhaps you have experienced a deep hurt that you are unable to let go of.

The Bible mentions forgiveness so often. It speaks about God's forgiveness toward us and our forgiveness toward one another. We have the assurance of God's Word that God forgives us our transgressions. God has freely given us that gift through his Son, Jesus. We have the hope of living free and forgiven through Christ. I invite you today to be gracious with yourself, as Christ is gracious to you.

May you be filled with the confidence and assurance that you are not only forgiven but also made pure. Go ahead: turn your face toward the sun!

Charlotte

PRAY

God, help me to turn my face toward you today. Forgive me and help me to forgive myself.

SAVOR

What do you need to release today so that you can turn your face toward God?

Week 9, Day 7

I WILL FOLLOW

Trust in the Lord with all your heart and lean not on your own understanding; in all your ways submit to him, and he will make your paths straight. —PROVERBS 3:5-6 (NIV)

Every summer we tackle at least one mountain climb. Generally, I don't lead, because we would probably never make it to the top. I need clear direction as well as a promise that the difficult journey will be worth the perseverance. Even though we need to take a slower pace and allow for breaks when I feel "done," we always eventually make it to the top.

Sometimes my beloved takes my hand, walks ahead of me, and encourages me during the steepest part of the climb, always having my best interests in mind. He leads well, with trail map in hand. I follow closely behind, because the path is often narrow and I can't see what is ahead. I know he would never mislead me intentionally, because he loves me.

My journey in following Jesus is much the same. Because I know that God loves me, I put my trust in him. I tell him that I want him to lead me and be Lord of my life. I listen to his instructions found in the Bible. I realize, over and over again, that I need a Savior, because I am weak in my resolve and too often mess up when I try to go it alone.

I can't see around the next bend and have no idea what lies ahead in my lifetime, but God knows. I will trust him because ultimately my journey leads to heaven. Every morning, I decide to stay on the path as I whisper, "Lead me, Jesus. I will follow."

Lovella

PRAY

Jesus, lead me today. Help me to trust you when I can't see far ahead. I commit to following you.

SAVOR

When in your life has it been most difficult to follow Jesus? When has the trail seemed easiest?

WEEK 10

Family Journeys
COUSINS UNITE

This past fall I traveled from British Columbia to a lakeside cabin in northern Michigan to join the female cousins on my mother's side for a reunion weekend.

Growing up in Ontario, we as cousins were close, gathering often at Grandpa and Grandma's house, running around the heavily laden tables in the basement or out in the yard while the aunts and uncles visited. In the evening we would pile together on a bed and listen while Grandma told Bible stories and stories of her childhood in Russia.

When I got married, we moved across Canada. Going back to Ontario was costly and only happened a few times. However, our connection as extended family remained strong through occasional letters and visits.

I am the oldest of the girls, and many of my younger cousins were still small children when I married, so this weekend gathering was a wonderful opportunity to get to know them as adults. Of the fourteen girl cousins, eleven were able to attend, as well as three of our five surviving aunts.

That reunion felt like a small foretaste of heaven. Joyful greetings filled the air as we spilled out of cars. There were huge hugs and lots of laughter and more than a few tears as we shared our lives with each other. Throughout the weekend we gathered in small and large groups, chatting around the table, enjoying the stillness of the lake, and walking through the autumn beauty. All the while, we reveled in the bond of family.

That reunion felt like a small foretaste of heaven.
Joyful greetings filled the air.

When I think of this time together, I am so grateful! I am grateful for Grandpa and Grandma, who had the courage and faith to leave family and friends and the only life they'd ever known in Russia to undertake the long journey to Canada, where everything was new and strange to them. They endured much hardship and poverty while struggling to adapt to this new home.

I am grateful for their strong faith, which they imparted to their children and grandchildren. My grandpa died the year I was born, but his faith legacy remains in the stories of his integrity and the quiet, godly influence he was in his community. My step-grandpa was also a shining example of love and faith to his adopted grandchildren. Grandma was a storyteller, and all her stories centered on God's leading and his faithfulness. We remember her for her strong faith and trust in God.

Although some of us have had rougher life journeys than others, all the cousins who gathered that weekend share a strong bond of faith. This faith shapes us and carries us through the highs and lows of our lives. I am convinced that we have Grandpa's and Grandma's prayers to thank for that.

I am grateful for the concept of family loyalty that was exemplified to us. We were taught that our faith came first, that offenses should be quickly forgiven, and that love for each other was not optional. At times there were disagreements among the family, but their love for each other was never in doubt. They supported and encouraged each other through thick and thin.

I am grateful for the prayers of my grandparents and extended family that have carried us this far and for the pledge we made to keep praying for each other. I am immeasurably grateful to God for this rich heritage.

Bev

Recipe
QUINOA CAKE BROWNIES

Yields 30 brownies

- 3 eggs
- ¾ cup / 175 ml coconut oil or butter
- ¾ cup / 175 ml sugar
- ¼ cup / 60 ml honey
- ½ cup / 125 ml milk
- 1 teaspoon / 5 ml vanilla
- 1¼ cup / 300 ml quinoa flour

- ¾ cup / 175 ml cocoa powder
- 2 teaspoons / 10 ml baking powder
- ½ teaspoon / 2 ml baking soda
- ½ teaspoon / 2 ml salt
- ¾ cup / 175 ml walnuts, crushed (optional)

1. Beat eggs and oil or butter with mixer.
2. Add sugar, honey, milk, and vanilla. Beat well.
3. Blend dry ingredients and add to liquids, mixing until smooth.
4. Stir in walnuts, if desired.

5. Pour into a 9 x 13-inch / 23 x 33-cm parchment-lined pan and bake at 350° F / 175° C for about 35–40 minutes.
6. Ice with chocolate icing, or serve with homemade caramel sauce (recipe follows) and a dollop of whipped cream or scoop of ice cream.

Caramel Sauce

- ⅓ cup / 75 ml butter
- ¾ cup / 175 ml brown sugar
- ½ cup / 125 ml whipping cream
- ½ tsp / 2 ml vanilla

1. In a saucepan, melt butter on medium heat.
2. Add brown sugar and bring to a boiling point.
3. Stir in whipping cream and vanilla. Turn heat to low and simmer for about 20 minutes
4. Cool sauce (it will thicken as it cools) and store in refrigerator until needed. Sauce can be reheated in microwave before serving, if desired.

With the emphasis on health and a growing number of people avoiding gluten, the quinoa flour in this recipe speaks to both! The texture is more like cake than brownies, but it has good flavor and can be dressed up or down as you desire.

Julie

Week 10, Day 1
SLICED BREAD

Blessed be the Lord, who daily bears us up;
God is our salvation. —PSALM 68:19 (ESV)

When I slice a loaf of bread, I am always struck by the fact that once sliced, a loaf of bread can never be whole again. I even feel a bit sorry that my deliberate action has irretrievably changed something whole and beautiful!

And yet a popular saying—"That's the greatest thing since sliced bread!"—makes the sliced loaf of bread a standard by which all other inventions are measured. Why? Because until the loaf of bread is sliced, it is useless. It is only when it is broken into pieces that it can fulfill its original purpose: to feed and nourish those who partake of it.

As we look back over our lives, we see that they are "sliced" into distinct seasons, experiences, and events. These slices have affected us emotionally, physically, and mentally. Some have filled us with joy, and some with sorrow or despair.

When I was diagnosed with rheumatoid arthritis, it crippled me with unbelievable pain. This slice of the loaf of my life was totally unexpected. Over time I surrendered that slice to God, and he worked something good out of my pain. Was it easy? No. But I learned patience, and I learned that God's peace is my strength. I experienced the wings of God's love that carried me when I could not walk. I learned that out of my suffering I was able to reach out to help others.

We have God's promise that if we trust him, he will work the slices of our lives together for our good. God will use the pieces of our lives to grow us in wisdom and strength and faith.

The years we have yet to live are like a whole, fresh loaf of bread. The life ahead of us has not yet been sliced. We do not know how the knife of time will slice the loaf of the years ahead. But God already knows, and we can safely put our trust in him. He will provide all that we will need!

Julie

PRAY
God, help me to trust you for my future. Nourish me with your love and salvation.

SAVOR
What "slices" from past years have been most difficult to swallow? How can you offer your past and your future to Jesus?

Week 10, Day 2
THE DOOR OF MY LIPS

Set a guard over my mouth, Lord; keep watch
over the door of my lips. —PSALM 141:3 (NIV)

Have you ever spoken thoughtlessly and then regretted it? You know what I mean, don't you? Have the words you were thinking ever come blurting out of your mouth before you've thought about what effect they would have on others?

When my children were young, I found that I would often feel frustrated as I got them ready for school in the morning. Rather than taking my time and thinking through how I could best motivate them without getting angry, I would snap at them. Sadly, it hurt them, and I often had to apologize.

Or have you ever shared something with someone that betrayed a confidence given to you to keep private? I have done it and regrettably lost a good friend in the process. A difficult lesson to learn indeed.

Paul writes in Ephesians 4:29, "Do not let any unwholesome talk come out of your mouths, but only what is helpful for building others up according to their needs, that it may benefit those who listen" (NIV). And Proverbs 12:18 tells us, "The words of the reckless pierce like swords, but the tongue of the wise brings healing" (NIV).

I find the following questions helpful when I think about what to say . . . and what not to say.

1. Is it kind? Would you say what you are saying if the person you are speaking about could hear you?
2. Is it necessary? Does the hearer need to know it?
3. Is it true? Do you know this for a fact, or is it hearsay?
4. Is it confidential? Is someone trusting you with this information?
5. Is it beneficial? Is it good for the person you are talking about and the person hearing it?

Our words have great power to build up. Think back on a time when someone spoke healing words to you, and say a prayer of thanks. May you use words today that become gifts to others, to edify, encourage, build up, and bring healing.

Charlotte

PRAY
God, guard my lips today. Give me words that build up and heal rather than tear down.

SAVOR
What kind of words do you hope to speak to those around you today?

Week 10, Day 3
MAGNOLIA TREE

---

*The God of all comfort . . . comforts us in all our troubles, so that
we can comfort those in any trouble with the comfort we ourselves
receive from God.* —2 CORINTHIANS 1:3-4 (NIV)

In April 2008, our wee granddaughter was born. Her name was
Hannah Shiloh, and it suited her just right. For months we had
known that she had a genetic condition that affected all her organs,
making it unlikely that she would live for more than a few hours after
birth. We cradled her briefly, admired her dark curls and soft skin, and
then we said our farewells. She was our visitor from heaven, and she
stayed only a short while. But our lives were touched forever.

When a child dies, the pain and the grief are indescribable. The
sense of loss that we felt as her family and friends was immense.
But the God who created us sees the big picture. He does not leave
us alone in our struggles. He brings comfort in so many ways. I can
testify to that.

At the time of Hannah's passing, we were given a little tree to plant
in her memory. It's a beautiful pink magnolia tree, and it chooses

to bloom on her birthday each year. I am always sad when the date comes and goes. And I always pause to think of the granddaughter who is missing from our little clan. In the middle of my sadness, the flowers make me smile. They are God's reminder that she is in his loving arms!

In 2 Corinthians 1:4, I am reminded again of how God provides strength. God surrounds us with friends and brings us through our difficult times. And because of the support that others have offered to me, I can now walk alongside those who are going through similar trials and offer empathy. God is our comfort, and we are his hands and feet in comforting others.

My magnolia tree is a reminder of our granddaughter's life, and it's also a reminder of God's comfort during a difficult time. God comforts us not to make us comfortable but to make us comforters.

Judy

PRAY

God, thank you for holding me in your arms during times of grief. Help me to pass on your comfort to others.

SAVOR

How have you experienced comfort from someone who was able to help you because they had gone through something similar?

Week 10, Day 4

CURVEBALLS

I pray that out of his glorious riches he may strengthen you with power through his Spirit in your inner being, so that Christ may dwell in your hearts through faith. And I pray that you, being rooted and established in love, may have power, together with all the Lord's holy people, to grasp how wide and long and high and deep is the love of Christ, and to know this love that surpasses knowledge—that you may be filled to the measure of all the fullness of God. —EPHESIANS 3:16-19 (NIV)

The phone rings: a quiet voice at the other end asks for help. An email arrives in my inbox: "Our daughter is in an induced coma . . . pray." An announcement is made at church: a young wife and mother has passed away. The husband says, "This is not how I would have written the last chapter."

How many curveballs can be thrown at us? Sometimes the number of curveballs in our lives seems overwhelming. Sometimes we question God: "Is this pain my punishment?"

I just spent a few days with some lifelong friends. One of my most cherished moments was when one of my friends said that we needed to sit down and pray together.

Right then and there, we took time to feel God's presence with us. We placed our hands on top of each other's hands in the center of the table, our arms like the spokes of a wheel joining us together as we quietly prayed.

Paul encourages all of us to come together as a family and to recognize God's source of power and love. He encourages us to continue staying in close contact with each other. Ravi Zacharias writes, "Prayer is not the means of bringing our will to pass but the means by which He brings our will into line to gladly receive His will."

We live in a world of curveballs—that is certain. But there is nothing more rewarding than to go out as Christ's church and share his love and mercy with others.

Marg

PRAY

God, help me to face the curveballs of life with you and with the support of your church. Help me to receive your will and your way without question.

SAVOR

How has prayer helped you face the curveballs of life?

Week 10, Day 5
FOCUS

I meditate on your precepts and consider your ways. I delight in your decrees; I will not neglect your word. —**PSALM 119:15-16 (NIV)**

We've all seen it—and maybe done it ourselves. Two friends get together for coffee to catch up . . . and one answers her cell phone when it rings. The other friend is left sitting there, listening in on the conversation or waiting while her friend finishes texting.

What about in church? With the Bible on many of our cell phones, more and more people are using those instead of bringing their actual Bibles to church. I have a Bible app on my phone too, but the distractions that come along with it can be problematic. I've noticed it a number of times in church: someone is using their cell phone to follow along with the Scripture reading . . . and then that person gets a text. Within a split second, the focus has changed from God's Word to someone else's.

Even if our phones are nowhere nearby, we're not immune from distraction. If you're like me, it can be difficult to stay focused during devotions. I pull out my Bible, pen, notebook, and sit in my quiet place, my intention much like the psalmist's. And then, like a slow infection, distractions creep in, drawing my attention away from the One I came to spend time with.

My parents set a faithful example for me in their daily reading of the Bible. I'm sure there were times they found themselves distracted, just as I often am. A number of years ago, I asked my dad what the key was to his faithful quiet time with the Lord. "Without it I'd be lost; it's my life," he said.

So I've been challenging myself to be more aware of distractions that creep in and things that pull me away from my focused time with God. He desires my undivided attention. It's in these times, when I make God my sole priority, that I've found the deeper riches in my relationship with him.

Kathy

PRAY

God, clear my mind and my heart of all the things that distract me from you. Thank you for spending time with me, and help me to focus on you.

SAVOR

What strategies can you use to focus better during times with God?

Week 10, Day 6
OPA'S TESTIMONY

Even to your old age and gray hairs I am he, I am he who will sustain you. I have made you and I will carry you; I will sustain you and I will rescue you. —ISAIAH 46:4 (NIV)

I was privileged to spend a brief holiday on Mayne Island off the southwest coast of British Columbia with my sister, Janet, and our dad. He is ninety-three years old and has been blessed with a long and healthy life.

It was the end of a beautiful day when he and I caught the ferry. We watched the sun go down on our way over to the island. Janet was there to meet us. The next day the three of us had a leisurely break-fast on the deck, and sat and talked for much of the morning as we watched the hummingbirds, butterflies, and bees among the flowers. Later we sat by the ocean, waded in the water, and watched the seals and otters at play.

Over and over again, Dad expressed his gratefulness to God: for the wonder of God's creation, for leading his parents to emigrate from the Ukraine and move to Canada when he was three years old, for being blessed to live in such a beautiful and peaceful place. He thanked God for his family, his friends, his home, and his health, and for salvation and the assurance of eternal life.

He recalled how God led in good times and difficult times, and he lives in humble gratitude for God's faithfulness to him. He never hesitates to share his love for God with his children, his grandchildren, and now, his great-grandchildren, who love to visit their "Opa."

As I grow older, my prayer is that I too will live with a grateful heart, proclaiming God's faithfulness to my children and grandchildren. As the psalmist says in Psalm 71, "Even when I am old and gray, do not forsake me, my God, till I declare your power to the next generation, your mighty acts to all who are to come" (v. 18 NIV).

Bev

PRAY

God, thank you for the witness of those who told me about you. Help me to tell of your power and your love to the next generation.

SAVOR

What stories of God's power in your life can you pass on to those who are younger, in faith or in age, than you?

Week 10, Day 7
FELLOWSHIP, NOT PERFECTION

Offer hospitality to one another without grumbling. Each of you should use whatever gift you have received to serve others, as faithful stewards of God's grace in its various forms. —1 PETER 4:9-10 (NIV)

Years ago, I attended a class in church about discerning the gifts that God has blessed us with, and we were encouraged to use what we enjoy doing to bless others. I enjoy spending time in my kitchen, baking and cooking, and I find much joy in sharing food with those who are too busy, who do not enjoy baking, or who are unable to do so.

Those of us who love to cook and bake can bless others at their place of work with a plate of freshly baked cookies, just in time for coffee break. We can invite people to our homes for a meal, which can be as simple as a bowl of soup and bread, or just for coffee and cookies. We should not worry about whether the furniture is dusted, or the dishes washed, or the toys put away. We want people to feel comfortable in our homes, and having a home that is warm and inviting will certainly do that. Overcoming the thought that we need a perfectly clean and beautifully decorated house allows us to open our hearts to fellowship with those we have invited into our home. The fellowship and sharing of God's love around the table is what really counts.

Volunteering to deliver meals to those in need is another way my husband, John, and I enjoy serving, sharing words of encouragement during those few moments we spend in their homes. We might be the only ones they see that day, and the joy on their faces is truly a blessing.

Jesus calls us to be hospitable, whether in our homes or away from them. It is serving unselfishly from the heart. Whether it's a smile, a hug, a listening ear, or a shared meal, do it joyfully and without complaining.

PRAY

God, help me to steward my gifts for your glory. Help me not to be perfect but to be faithful.

SAVOR

What does true hospitality look like to you? How can you offer fellowship, not perfection, to someone today?

WEEK 11

Family Journeys
ANNA'S LONGING FOR HEAVEN

My grandmother, Anna Niebuhr, was born into a wealthy family in Ukraine. In the late 1920s, under the Stalin regime, life became almost unbearable for anyone who owned factories and estates, as they were forced to give up everything and threatened with exile as well. My grandmother's family eventually moved to the easternmost part of Russia. In 1930, they fled by night across the Amur River to China. My grandmother, who had just married, stayed behind in Russia.

I imagine she may have later wondered if she made the right decision, as the years that followed brought about many a trial. About a

Above: Anna and her son, Peter Janzen (Anneliese's father), in 1944 after losing the rest of their family.

year after she was wed, she gave birth to a son, who died in infancy. Next came my father, and then another son, who died as a toddler in 1937 because she could not get medical help. In the same year, her husband was imprisoned for unknown reasons. He was executed a year later.

My grandmother was left alone with one young son: my father. Together they braved the hardships of the times.

When World War II broke out, they were living in a Mennonite village in Ukraine, where there was still a remnant of people who had not been able to leave the country. When the German army came through, they recognized these people as being German and took them into their protection. My grandmother was put to work mending uniforms. One day, as she was mending gloves, putting her hand into each one in order to sew a tear, she realized too late that her wedding ring had stayed in one of the gloves. I can only imagine her sadness.

My grandmother was left alone with one young son: my father. Together they braved the hardships of the times.

This was not an easy time, but they were grateful for the food and shelter they received and for being able to get to Germany via the army. In 1947, Anna and her son, my father, left on a ship from Germany to Paraguay. There they met up with the rest of the family who had fled to China and then to Paraguay seventeen years earlier, with help from Mennonite Central Committee.

When I was growing up, my grandmother lived with us, her only son and his family. I have numerous memories of time spent in her room—combing her hair, talking about Russia, playing guitar, and learning German songs. I wish now that I had paid better attention to her stories. The thing that stands out about her was her deep longing for heaven, which had become more dear to her through the sorrows of this world.

As a young adult in Paraguay, my father learned that before his father married Anna, he had been widowed and had left a son with a sister. Having thought he was alone all these years, my father was deeply moved to realize he had a half-brother in Russia, whom he had memories of from his childhood. While in Russia, they thought they were cousins. My father made it his goal to find his only brother.

More than thirty-five years after they were separated, my father and his half-brother were reunited in Canada. As they talked, they realized that, without their knowledge, they had married in the same year and even had their first three children in the exact same years. Then, after being able to get to know each other again, both went to their heavenly home in 2007.

My grandmother's longing for and assurance of heaven is the best gift she gave us, as it now reminds me of our ultimate meeting place, where there will be no more goodbyes. I'm looking forward to introducing her to her large family!

Anneliese

Recipe
BUTTER TARTS

Yields 24 mini tarts

Filling
- 2 tablespoons / 30 ml butter, room temperature
- 1 cup / 250 ml brown sugar
- 1 egg

- ½ teaspoon / 2 ml salt
- 1 teaspoon / 5 ml vanilla
- 1 cup / 250 ml golden raisins (optional)

1. Beat butter, brown sugar, and egg together until creamy.
2. Add salt and vanilla.

If using raisins, pour boiling water over them to plump them. Allow to stand for 5 minutes. Drain well. Do not add to filling mixture, but set aside to fill unbaked tart shells.

Pastry

- 1⅔ cup / 400 ml flour, plus additional for forming pastry
- ¾ teaspoon / 4 ml salt
- ⅔ cup / 150 ml lard
- 4 tablespoons / 60 ml cold water

1. Combine flour and salt in a medium bowl.
2. Using a pastry blender, cut lard into flour and salt mixture until it forms pea-sized lumps.
3. Add cold water to mixture. Using a fork, stir until dough starts to come together. It may seem dry at this point.
4. Pull dough together with your hands and shape dough into a ball.
5. Sprinkle some flour on counter or pastry mat and roll out dough until fairly thin.
6. Lightly dip a cup or round cookie cutter in flour and cut out dough in shapes large enough to line the cups of a mini muffin or mini tart pan. There should be enough to make 24 tarts.
7. Line cups of pan with pastry rounds.
8. Divide raisins equally between unbaked tart shells, if desired.
9. Pour equal amounts of butter tart filling into each shell.
10. Bake at 375° F / 205° C for 18–20 minutes. Let rest in pan for 5 minutes before removing to cooling rack.

Butter tarts are a true Canadian treat. A perfect butter tart is dependent on its flaky, crisp pastry and its buttery, sweet filling. Butter tart connoisseurs differ in opinion about whether to add raisins or to use the filling by itself. You can decide which you prefer.

TIP

For a raisin-nut filling, replace ½ cup / 125 ml of the raisins with ½ cup / 125 ml chopped nuts.

Kathy

Week 11, Day 1
SCARECROWS

Like a scarecrow in a cucumber field, their idols cannot speak; they must be carried because they cannot walk. Do not fear them; they can do no harm nor can they do any good. —JEREMIAH 10:5 (NIV)

I have the pleasure of looking out my kitchen window every morning to see the beauty of windblown tassels in the cornfields. One morning when I looked out, I gasped. Who was standing out there staring at me?

Suddenly I realized it was a scarecrow. I smiled at myself and remembered a time long ago when my grandparents erected scarecrows in their garden. I remember learning as a child that when a scarecrow is erected, the crows believe that it is a real person and leave the field alone.

A scarecrow has no ability to hurt anyone or anything. It has absolutely no power and no life. It can frighten but it cannot harm. Our enemy, the devil, is like a scarecrow—trying to frighten us away from Christ. We know that if we put Christ first in our life, the enemy cannot prevail.

What are the scarecrows in your life? Is it fear of failing to succeed? Fear can paralyze us. Is it anxiety? A diagnosis of terminal illness? Is it fear of the future?

In Jeremiah 10, we learn that the people of Judah wanted to know their future and so they used horoscopes. They wanted to know which mistakes they could avoid in life and how to climb the ladder to prosperity. In the verse above, we see Jeremiah the prophet warning the people of Judah about their irrational fears.

The beauty of this truth is that scarecrows have no power. So how are you going to handle life when a scarecrow pops up in your life? God promises to guide you and knows your future. He will reveal the future to you and will walk with you as the future unfolds. Let's take God's Word and allow the warm rays of sunshine fill our lives. Let's stand firm on God's promises and carry those useless scarecrows out of our lives.

Marg

PRAY

God, deliver me from fear and anxiety. Turn my eyes from my scarecrows to your awesome power.

SAVOR

What are the scarecrows in your life?

Week 11, Day 2
GRACIOUS RECEIVERS

Therefore encourage one another and build each other up,
just as in fact you are doing. —1 THESSALONIANS 5:11 (NIV)

Kind words, affirmation, encouragement—I think we often under-estimate the power behind these things. "How are you, really?" "I'm praying for you." "I have a verse to share with you." "Want to go for coffee?" Such encouraging words are like good medicine for a tired soul. They bring comfort, and they renew hope.

I personally have received this kind of care from friends along life's way. During her college years, our youngest daughter was diagnosed with epilepsy. I recall many friends calling to share our concern and pray with us. We received verses and beautiful cards with words of encouragement. Coffee times with friends helped carry us through those difficult days of uncertainty. I know that it pleases the heart of God when we reach out to one another with a truly caring spirit. "Gracious words are like a honeycomb, sweetness to the soul and health to the body" (Proverbs 16:24 ESV).

I believe that God also wants each of us to be givers of kind words, affirmation, and encouragement. You may need to hear that you are loved and being lifted up in prayer today. You may need a friend to remind you today that no matter what your situation or circumstance, God cares for you. He loves you.

Scripture encourages us to use kind words and build each other up. May God help us to be generous givers of encouragement . . . and also gracious receivers.

Kathy

PRAY

God, give me the grace to give—and receive—encouragement today.

SAVOR

Think of a time that you received encouragement from a friend. Imagine passing on those words to someone else today.

Week 11, Day 3
THE LEGACY WE LEAVE

I will extol you, my God and King, and bless your name forever and ever. Every day I will bless you and praise your name forever and ever. Great is the Lord, and greatly to be praised, and his greatness is unsearchable. One generation shall commend your works to another, and shall declare your mighty acts. —PSALM 145:1-4 (ESV)

Think back to the most precious birthday gift you ever received. It might have been a shiny red bicycle when you were a child, or a carefully thought-out gift of time. The best memories our sons have of time spent with their grandpa include going out for doughnuts together or working with him on secret projects that would become gifts for family members.

If you have such a special memory, you will understand how my beloved felt as he held our brand-new grandson, born in the early morning on his birthday! This new little lad not only shares a birthday with his grandpa; he also bears the name of his great-grandpa, my beloved's father.

Dad passed away when our sons were thirteen and fifteen years old. They have been without their grandpa longer than they had him in their lives. But the memories and the legacy that my father-in-law left are still clear.

We have one lifetime to leave a legacy that speaks of the greatness and mighty acts of our heavenly Father. We can commend God's works to our children and grandchildren, or we can choose to remain silent. If we praise our Father and bless his name forever and ever, the next generation will remember.

Lorella

PRAY

Lord, thank you for the blessing of new life. Help us take every opportunity we have to speak truth and love into children's lives. Grant us wisdom to pass on the gift of faith to the next generation.

SAVOR

How are you commending the works of God to the next generation?

Week 11, Day 4
RAG RUG BEAUTY

Therefore, if anyone is in Christ, the new creation has come:
The old has gone, the new is here! —2 CORINTHIANS 5:17 (NIV)

Rag rugs have always fascinated me. As a little girl, I would sit and watch my mother cut strips of fabric from old shirts, pants, and dresses that were too worn to wear anymore. She'd sit by the woodstove, where she could stay warm as she worked. With nimble fingers, using a hook that had been carved out of wood by my dad, she would create a beautiful rug.

Her rugs were works of art. Each rug was unique because of the different fabrics she used. I remember my dad's faded blue-checked shirt, cut up into strips that she then sewed together and rolled into a ball, waiting to be woven into a rug.

We used these rugs all over the house—by the sink, by the oven, and any place where you could warm your feet as you did household chores. My favorite one was beside my bed; it made it easier to get out of bed on those cold, frosty mornings.

These memories take me to what Jesus does for us. He takes the old, ragged, and worn pieces of our lives and weaves them into beautiful new works of art. The ragged and worn parts could be the loss of a job, a struggle with health issues, or the feeling of not being valued. If we give these struggles to God, he will use them and weave them into something beautiful in our lives.

That is the most amazing weaving that I can think of. How thankful I am that God doesn't just throw out the worn-out parts of our lives. Instead, he takes them and creates something entirely new. The old has gone, and the new is here—not because the old is destroyed, but because the old has actually become the new.

Wait for the Lord and keep his way, and he will exalt you to inherit the land; you will look on when the wicked are cut off. —PSALM 37:34 (ESV)

D o you find that when you pray for something, you sometimes get impatient for the Lord to act? It is not uncommon for us as believers to get impatient. I know that I do, especially if it is something that I have been praying for a long time. To "wait for the Lord," as the psalmist says, means you are expecting something wonderful to happen with confidence and hope that surely God will answer.

So why does it sometimes seem that God is silent?

During times of waiting, I can either become anxious and impatient—or I can allow God to transform me from the inside out. His desire is to change my heart and character to become more like his. He wants me to learn to trust him. (I must admit that I am not fully there yet.)

It is during those times of waiting that I have become more familiar with God's grace, love, and power in my life. When I come to that place of surrender and of allowing God to be in control, then I truly experience his peace, which passes all understanding. When I try to take control, it just brings more anxiety. (Trust me; I know!)

I am trying to learn to embrace the process of this journey God has me on. I am trying to rely on his power as I wait for my prayers to be answered in better ways than I ever dreamed possible. I am choosing to focus my attention on God rather than on the challenges that lie before me.

"Wait for the Lord," the psalmist tells us. "Be strong and take heart and wait for the Lord" (Psalm 27:14 NIV). I want to encourage you to surrender and trust the Lord. Waiting for him is not easy, and it's tempting to get impatient as we wait. But we know that God's peace can calm our impatient spirits.

Charlotte

PRAY

God, help me to wait patiently on your will. Jesus, thank you for waiting with me.

SAVOR

What prayers are you waiting for God to answer? Turn the waiting period on these prayers over to him.

Week 11, Day 6
WATER MY SPIRIT

---

*And he said to me, "It is done! I am the Alpha and the Omega, the
beginning and the end. To the thirsty I will give from the spring of
the water of life without payment.* —**REVELATION 21:6 (ESV)**

Some friends gave me potted impatiens as a gift. When the plant
came to me, its rich green leaves crowded for space in a profusion
of deep pink blooms. Over the past months, this plant has bloomed
and bloomed, putting ever so many smiles on my face.

I love this plant. I know there are healthier potted impatiens than
this one, but let me tell you why I love it.

I do not have a green thumb, so plants have to have some inner
resilience of their own. At times, leaf and bloom of the impatiens hung
down, a result of "drought" in the pot when I forgot to water. But
when I mercifully remembered the needed water, the impatiens happily
raised up and continued to delight me.

Then came the day when I thought I surely had lost it. Leaves and
flowers fell off, and the plant looked hopeless. But I was reluctant to
throw it out—perhaps because of guilt and the knowledge that I had

neglected it. On a whim, I took it inside and gave it some water. One last chance.

And it returned to life! Water revived it. Amazing, isn't it?

My plant needs water to grow. How often and how faithfully it is given water determines the growth rate, somewhere between surviving and thriving.

So it is with my spirit. It has a God-given resilience, but whether it survives or thrives is up to me. How faithful am I in spending time in God's Word? How often do I lift my voice in prayerful relationship with him?

I think of times in my life when, through neglect, I have allowed my spirit to droop and even come close to dying. But it is never too late to drink of the water of life. It is never too late for us to be restored to health. We, like my impatiens, can thrive once again!

Julie

PRAY
Water of life, revive me with your love.

SAVOR
How can you allow God to revive your spirit today?

I will sing to the Lord as long as I live; I will sing praise to my God while I have being. May my meditation be pleasing to him, for I rejoice in the Lord. —PSALM 104:33-34 (ESV)

What stands out to me the most about holidays when I was growing up is music, especially songs associated with Christmas and Easter. Russian was the first language used in the churches we attended. By the time I was in high school, our Russian Baptist church was bilingual. Our Christmas and Easter services rang out with carols and hymns sung in Russian and English. Our youth choir would practice for weeks before each of these holidays in order to prepare a cantata for the Sunday evening service. Our cantatas were in English.

On Christmas Eve, the youth would always go caroling. We would start at the apartment building a couple of doors down from the church, where my maternal grandmother (*Babushka*) lived, along with a few other widows from our congregation. We would then carol at senior homes where church members were being cared for. We'd sing in English and Russian at these homes.

Christmas morning and Easter morning we would have an early breakfast at our maternal Babushka's apartment and then walk to our church. On Easter, the greeting of "*Kristos Voskress*!" (Christ is risen!) would be on everyone's lips, along with the response: "*Voistina Voskress*!" (He is risen indeed!) It was guaranteed that we'd sing "Low in the Grave He Lay" on Easter morning, with no one holding back. To this day I expect to be able to sing that hymn on Easter. I miss those days in my home church.

God has used music to speak to me in a personal way through the years and to prompt me in my growth with him. When I wake up in the middle of the night, a hymn or worship song is often going through my mind. I like waking up that way. I loved singing songs about Jesus to our children when they were young. Music adds a special joy in my life, and I'm happy to sing all year long. To this day, whenever my extended family gets together, we end up singing a few songs together in Russian and English.

When God calls me home, I hope to go out singing!

Ellen

PRAY

God, thank you for the gift of music. Give me a song to glorify you today.

SAVOR

How has music strengthened your relationship with God?

WEEK 12

Family Journeys
THE LAST TEA PARTY

The year was 1926, and the family had gathered at the home of the grandparents in South Russia. Grandmother wanted a photo of the grandchildren, dressed in all their finery and having a tea party. It was the year that my mother was born, so she is missing from the photograph of all the cousins. I doubt they knew it would be the last time they all sat around the table together.

Due to political upheaval, the family was soon scattered. Some left for Canada. My mother's family followed several years later, and her grandparents were exiled to Siberia. All they had left of their time together were the memories, the traditions, and the photograph.

Above: Judy's mother's cousins in the home of their grandparents in southern Russia in 1926.

There is something special about everyone gathering around the table at Grandma's house. It's where cousins become good friends, where favorite family foods are shared, and where stories from the old days are told time and time again. Several decades later, cousins were again gathering around the table. I have fond memories of time spent at my grandmother's table. In those days, the adults ate first. What a novel concept! Once they were finished with their meal, the table was set again for all of us children, the cousins. The food was every bit as good as the meal at the first seating.

Sunday supper always included *Zwieback* (double-decker buns), *Kotletten* (cold meatballs), potato salad, Jell-O salad, and an assortment of Grandma's trademark cookies. In the summer, Grandma also organized a cousin picnic, and we would have watermelon and *Rollkuchen* (fried bread).

When my own children arrived, time spent at Grandma's table was always special for them. She knew exactly what each of the grandchildren enjoyed eating, and prepared it for them. And she always had treats.

There is something special about everyone gathering around the table at Grandma's house.

I have no idea how this all happened so quickly, but now *I* am the grandmother and the cousins are gathering around *my* table. I love to have the family come home for all those special occasions. We celebrate birthdays and other milestones in life. Who better to share those moments with than family? We bought a larger dining room table so that we can all fit around it. There is no second seating! It is full, but we always seem to find room to add one more spot. Usually the cousins run off to play after we eat, while the adults take their time dining and chatting. They all return for dessert!

Just as my great-grandmother in Russia did so long ago, I enjoy having my grands around the table. I began hosting tea parties with the oldest granddaughters many years ago on Valentine's Day. When their brother arrived, he did not want to be left out. Now they all come and we have a grand tea party, whatever the occasion may be.

We never know what tomorrow may bring, but as long as it is today, we will celebrate our family. Gathering around the table with family is about cementing family ties, carrying on traditions, and caring for each other.

Judy

Recipe
RUSSIAN TEA COOKIES

Yields 36–48 cookies

- 1 cup / 250 ml butter
- ½ cup / 125 ml powdered sugar, plus additional for coating cookies
- 1 teaspoon / 5 ml vanilla

- 2½ cups / 625 ml sifted flour
- ¼ teaspoon / 1 ml salt
- ¾ cup / 175 ml nuts, finely chopped

1. Cream butter and sugar.
2. Add vanilla, sifted flour, salt, and nuts. Mix well.
3. Form into small balls.
4. Place on an ungreased cookie sheet. If you want, you can flatten them a bit.
5. Bake in a preheated 400° F / 205° C oven for 11–14 minutes, or until bottoms are lightly browned.
6. While still warm, roll in powdered sugar.
7. After cool, roll again in powdered sugar.

Russian tea cookies are a family favorite. They melt in your mouth. I like to make them small enough so that they can be eaten in one bite. They make a very nice cookie for formal teas. They are also a great choice for Christmas, as they look like snowballs.

TIP
If you make smaller balls, watch the bake time carefully, as they will be done sooner.

Elle

Week 12, Day 1
IF JESUS SHOWED UP

*The King will reply, "Truly I tell you, whatever you did for one of
the least of these brothers and sisters of mine, you did for me."*
—MATTHEW 25:40 (NIV)

What would you do / if Jesus came to your house / to spend some time with you?"

These are the words of a song I heard playing on the radio today. It's a song from long ago, and one that I know well. For some reason it caught my attention today, and the song's question lingers in my thoughts. What would I do if Jesus came to my house today?

Would I serve him a delicious meal, plated up beautifully and prepared with care?

Would I be able to honestly say I had been reading his book faithfully and doing what it teaches?

Would I rearrange my busy schedule and take time to sit and listen to him?

Would I invite him back? Or would I be ashamed of and embarrassed by anything in my life?

Of course I would want to do all these things—and I'd want to do more, too. Matthew 25 reminds us that Jesus does come to spend time with us; it's just that most of us don't recognize him. He comes to us as the "least of these," and we'd do well to look for him in our sisters and brothers who are poor and needy. To truly give Jesus my best, I need to strive to be more attentive to the needs of others and to reach out a helping hand when needed.

I will have to stand before him and give an account of my life. I have been entrusted with abilities and time for furthering God's kingdom, whether that means helping someone financially or offering a listening ear. He is my Master, and I am his servant. I must stay in fellowship with him by reading his Word and applying it daily in my life.

This is my prayer, then: that I will be obedient in doing God's will. I want to live my life in such a way that I would not be ashamed to have Jesus come to spend some time with me. If Jesus shows up to me today, I want to be ready.

PRAY

Jesus, thank you for coming to spend time with us even when we don't recognize you.

SAVOR

How can you give Jesus your best today?

Week 12, Day 2
SCORCHED

The Lord will guide you always; he will satisfy your needs in a sun-scorched land and will strengthen your frame. You will be like a well-watered garden, like a spring whose waters never fail. —ISAIAH 58:11 (NIV)

There have been dry seasons in my walk with God. Perhaps you can identify. Your prayers seem to go no farther than the ceiling. Reading your Bible seems more a chore than a delight.

I experienced this after my mom died. I had difficulty concentrating on anything, and my walk with God was characterized by lethargy and lack of motivation. A few years later, we experienced some serious misunderstanding in our church, which brought us much pain and despair. We cried out to God, but our prayers seemed to no avail. We struggled to find some meaning in it all.

So do you give up and resign yourself to living in a drought-ravaged land? Or do you get up and walk until you find water and lush growth again?

I know from experience that walking by yourself does not work. You trudge along day by day, and just when you think you'll find your way out of that dry place, you are back where you started.

The more reliable option is to remember God's promises and to choose to believe that God is walking beside you. Psalm 23 offers this lovely promise: "Even though I walk through the darkest valley, I will fear no evil, for you are with me; your rod and your staff, they comfort me" (v. 4 NIV).

There will be deserts and dark valleys along life's journey. The important thing is to remember God is with us during those times. He promises to never leave us or forsake us. That includes those dark and dry times.

When we invite God to walk with us through the desert, he will be our shade in the heat of the noonday sun and provide food and water for our hungry and parched souls. He will lead us to green pastures, restore our souls, and turn the dry desert into a well-watered garden.

Bev

PRAY

God, lead me through the desert times so that I might come out on the other side, nourished and watered by you.

SAVOR

What Scriptures have carried you through the desert times?

Week 12, Day 3
CELEBRATING UNITY

May the God of endurance and encouragement grant you to live in such harmony with each other, in accord with Christ Jesus. —ROMANS 15:5 (ESV)

Someone once asked our group of Mennonite Girls Can Cook authors what our biggest challenge has been. I think they were asking how ten women could agree on how to do a cookbook.

As the spokesperson for this group, I had to really think. What was our biggest challenge? Was it picking the recipes? Was it whose bun or *Borscht* recipe we should include? Did we squabble behind the scenes? Was there an underlying note of discontent that we kept out of the public arena?

I can say with a smile and a thankful heart that we have been blessed by the Lord with unity. He alone began this work among us, and he alone knew from the first recipe post that we would have opportunities to share something worthwhile with our readers. God already knew that we would have the incredible privilege of sharing the royalties from our books with those in need.

We are ten sisters in the Lord who stand shoulder to shoulder. We share a common passion of sharing our family recipes, encouraging hospitality, and making a difference in the lives of those who are hungry.

One of our most special times together was when we asked God's blessing on our meal at a celebration dinner with our husbands. Charlotte prayed in both High German and Low German, languages most of us heard in our homes. Ellen then prayed in Russian, the mother tongue of the land our ancestors all traveled through. We then stood and sang the doxology in four-part harmony. It was a beautiful time of giving God praise for what he has done.

God has blessed our friendship. I can honestly say that our biggest challenge has been finding enough days on our calendars to all be together.

Praise God from whom all blessings flow!

Lovella

PRAY

Thank you, God, for sisterhood in Jesus. Make us instruments of your love for others.

SAVOR

How do you experience unity in Christ with other women? How can you nurture such holy friendships?

Week 12, Day 4
GOOD SOIL

The seed falling on good soil refers to someone who hears the word and understands it. This is the one who produces a crop, yielding a hundred, sixty or thirty times what was sown. —MATTHEW 13:23 (NIV)

My daughter and her husband recently moved into a house with a large yard. They were excited to learn how to grow a beautiful lawn and spruce up the old flower beds. It was a lot of work, but they were quite happy with the initial results.

Before long, however, our daughter told me that weeds, weeds, and more weeds were coming up. "Why is it that we have to give so much attention to the plants that we want to grow and yet these weeds just come from nowhere and take over?" she asked with exasperation. Then she told me how this had been a spiritual lesson of sorts for her.

In the parable of the sower, Jesus told of a farmer who threw his seeds on the ground. Not all of them grew to produce fruit. Thorns and thistles grew up to choke out the good seed.

It is frustrating to see that, just like the weeds, sin needs no encouragement. It can pop up in the most unexpected places and take over.

It's a part of our fallen world—a world in which we need to be alert and ready to weed out sin so that the good seed can grow.

I'm not a gardener, but I know one thing: weeding just gets harder if you ignore it. If I allow the weeds to take over, there will be fewer good things to harvest.

Anneliese

PRAY

Lord, allow me to recognize the weeds and the thorns that choke the good seed in the soil of my heart. Help me to be persistent in allowing you to weed and water for a good harvest.

SAVOR

What weeds do you need to deal with in your life right now? Imagine the lovely plants that can grow when you deal with them!

Week 12, Day 5
BE RIGHT THERE

A friend loves at all times, and a brother is
born for adversity. —PROVERBS 17:17 (ESV)

What kind of friend am I, really? A recent devotional in *Our Daily Bread* was entitled "Be a Stander." The author, Bill Crowder, writes that a friend who is a "stander" will stay close in times of trouble. A friend who bolts at the first sign of trouble isn't really much of a friend.

How blessed I am to have good friends who have stood beside me when trouble has come. I often think of the ones who stood by us when my husband faced cancer more than thirty years ago. Fifteen years ago, friends came and showed us how to farm when we had no clue. And friends stood shoulder to shoulder with us when we put our parents to rest.

My dear friend Kathy once said that her parents taught her by example. She told me that when they knew someone was in trouble, her parents would always say, "We'll be right there."

Now Kathy is an example of that approach to friendship as well. I see her example in my own life. Several years ago she displayed the most thoughtful way of showing me she was praying for me through a family crisis. She dropped off a beautiful gift basket. It was filled with little gifts that she had carefully thought through, including tissues for tears, chocolates for comfort, notebooks for recording prayers, and candles to light a dark night.

When I see her live out her friendship like that, I want to be that kind of a friend—the kind that says, "I'll be right there!" When my friends face difficult times, will I be a stander—one who stays right beside them? Or will I bolt?

Even though I desire to be the kind of friend that the Bible talks about, the reality is that I am human and fail my friends more often than I should. There is no friend like Jesus. He bears all our griefs. He never leaves us. He never bolts when the going gets tough, and he is the ultimate example of the friend who stands close to us no matter what happens.

Lorella

PRAY

Dear Lord, help me to be the kind of friend who doesn't run when my friends are in need. Give me the courage to stand by them, the wisdom to know what to say.

SAVOR

Who has been a model "stander" for you? How can you stand beside a friend today?

Week 12, Day 6
NEVER GIVE UP

But now, this is what the Lord says—he who created you, Jacob, he who formed you, Israel: "Do not fear, for I have redeemed you; I have summoned you by name; you are mine. When you pass through the waters, I will be with you; and when you pass through the rivers, they will not sweep over you. When you walk through the fire, you will not be burned; the flames will not set you ablaze. For I am the Lord your God, the Holy One of Israel, your Savior." —ISAIAH 43:1-3 (NIV)

A few years ago, someone shared this Scripture with me in such a way that it has never left me. My friend suggested that I fill in the verses with my own name. "Do not fear, for I have redeemed you, Marg; I have summoned you by name; you, Marg, are mine."

When I put my own name into the verses, it becomes a powerful lesson in trusting God. God never promised us an easy way out. Many times, believers think that life will be easy because they have taken a new step of faith.

We know that we will go through difficult times in our lives, but if we invite the Lord to go with us, it will make our load lighter. God did not say that he would keep us from difficult times. When we go through hardships, we can drown or we can grow stronger. God promises that he will protect us, just as a father cares for his child. "Do not be afraid, for I am with you," God promises (Isaiah 43:5 NIV).

God gives renewed hope to all who are going through difficult situations.

Marg

PRAY

God, thank you for your promise to be with me all the time, through all kinds of hardship.

SAVOR

Add your name to these verses. How does it change how you hear this promise from God?

Week 12, Day 7
COME TO THE TABLE

And the angel said to me, "Write this: Blessed are those who are
invited to the marriage supper of the Lamb." And he said to me,
*"These are the true words of God." —*REVELATION 19:9 (ESV)

Growing up in a Mennonite home, I understood early on the importance of the table. Fellowship happened around our table—not only for the family but also for the many guests who entered the home.

Guests were never invited to a table that was not covered with a beautiful tablecloth and china dishes. It is amazing to me that my mother-in-law, who fled the Ukraine in World War II with three young children and lost almost everything she owned, managed to keep with her a tablecloth that belonged to her mother and grandmother. She gave me that tablecloth shortly before she died.

Throughout the Bible, writers often refer to the importance of the table to the life of faith. Abraham offered food to his divine guests. Jesus made many references to food and feasts in his parables. He multiplied loaves and fishes, and he shared a last supper with his disciples—a meal that we still partake of when we come to the communion table. The early believers met daily to share their evening meal.

There is, however, a very special supper spoken of that is yet in the future: a celebration supper in heaven for Jesus and his bride. What a magnificent table that will be!

The invitations have been sent out to every person, but there is an RSVP required. Have you responded to the invitation? And have you offered the invitation to others?

Julie

PRAY

God, thank you for the invitation to the wedding feast of the Lamb. Help me to extend the invitation to my friends and neighbors.

SAVOR

What memories do you have of gathering around the table for food and fellowship? How do those memories connect to the marriage supper of the Lamb?

WEEK 13

Family Journeys
LEAVE A GOOD FOOTPRINT BEHIND

I have been thinking a lot lately about my maternal grandfather, who was born in 1899 in the Ukraine to a Mennonite family. He was a quiet man, not given to many words, and he died many years ago. But simply who he was has left a deep imprint on who I am.

My grandpa did not have an easy life. We know very little of my grandfather's growing-up years, as he was reluctant to talk about his early life. He was the youngest child of his parents' large family; the older siblings were already on their own when he came along. His mother had become blind before he was born, and she never saw her youngest son's face.

Above: Julie's grandfather Franz Reinke in his 1928 passport photograph.

When he was twenty-one, his mother died, and then also his father and brother from typhoid fever. He cared for his father and brother, and when they died he realized he himself had contracted the dreaded plague. Now without his parents, he had only one goal in mind: to walk to Greunfeld, the village where his fiancée, Helene, lived. By the time he reached her door, he was so ill he was delirious.

Helene, my grandmother, nursed him back to health and they were married shortly afterward. A friend from his own village was able to get a warning message to him that he should not return, as the Russian authorities were looking for him to force him into the army.

When my grandmother was pregnant with her fourth child, they immigrated to Canada, raising their children on a farm in Saskatchewan. My grandparents then followed their two oldest daughters, who had married and moved to British Columbia.

I had the privilege of growing up next door to my grandparents. We lived on adjoining farms. Beside the fence dividing our cow pasture and Mom's large garden was a long, well-trodden path between our two homes. Some of my first memories include being carried by my mom along the path to visit her parents. When I was old enough to go by myself, I so clearly remember that pretty walk to visit them. In the summer, Mom's dahlia bushes were taller than I was.

My grandfather was a quiet man, not given to many words, but he has left a deep imprint on who I am.

Grandpa never lost the child within him. He was always very curious. Every Christmas morning, we kids would get up at the crack of dawn to see our gifts under the tree. Without fail, a few minutes later, Grandpa—who had been watching to see the house lights come on—would be at the door to see what we got. He was almost as excited as we were!

My grandfather was strong and dependable, and the love that shone from his soft brown eyes spoke volumes. He worked hard to make a living but never complained. He was content with the simple things of life. Grandpa simply lived his faith, and he left a deep spiritual impression on my life. The one constant thing in his life was his faith, which never wavered. He loved to pray and he loved his Bible, enjoying nothing more than discussing doctrinal issues. Many nights I would lie awake in bed and listen to the adult conversations going on in the kitchen.

Franz Reinke's Russian passport.

There is a German expression that says "*Lass eine gute Spur zurück*": Leave a good footprint behind. I think we are often totally unaware of the "footprints" we are leaving behind, or who will see them and follow in them. I don't believe my grandfather was ever aware that anyone was watching him. He was a very humble man—he reflected the true kind of humility that is totally unaware of itself. But so often it is not the footprints we purposefully set down in the soft sands of life that are observed by others. Rather, time and again, the footprints that matter are the ones to which we never give a second thought.

I'm grateful for the authentic, exemplary lives of people like my grandpa, who have left solid footprints that lead others along the right path.

Julie

Recipe
STRAWBERRY RHUBARB JAM

Yields 4 cups / 1 L

- 6 cups / 1.5 L rhubarb, finely chopped
- 3 cups / 750 ml sugar
- ¼ cup / 60 ml orange or apple juice

- 1 (3-ounce / 90-g) package strawberry-flavored gelatin

1. Combine chopped rhubarb, sugar, and juice.
2. Stir well and allow to sit for several hours.
3. Bring to a boil over medium heat.
4. Reduce heat and simmer for 12 minutes, stirring continuously.
5. Remove from heat and stir in gelatin.
6. Pour into sterile jars that hold 1 cup / 250 ml and refrigerate. This jam can also be frozen.

Strawberry rhubarb jam is like spring in a jar! This recipe adds strawberry flavor to the rhubarb jam by using strawberry-flavored gelatin; this comes in handy when the rhubarb is ready for the picking but the strawberries are still far from ripe. Spread it on toast, buttermilk biscuits, freshly baked rolls, or use as a topping for ice cream.

Judy

Week 13, Day 1
HOPE DEFERRED

For in this hope we were saved. But hope that is seen is no hope at all.
Who hopes for what they already have? —ROMANS 8:24 (NIV)

When my children were young, I sometimes prayed for them to be placed in a certain class for the next year. One particular year, when my "hope" did not come true, I talked to the principal . . . only to find out later that my child would have been changed without my intervention. But I was too impatient to wait and see!

As moms, we may know what a good situation is for our kids, but sometimes we need to trust. It is hard to know when to wait and when to do something.

With a promise of being blessed with future generations, Abraham and Sarah set out in anticipation for a country God would show them. But as the years went by and there was no child, Sarah resigned herself to the life of one who would never be a mother. Her resignation led her to take things into her own hands by planning a way to raise a family by a surrogate mother, or maidservant. If Sarah had waited on God, the story would have turned out much differently.

As women, we understand how Sarah would lose all hope. Proverbs tells us plainly that "hope deferred makes the heart sick" (13:12 NIV).

I don't know why God did not give Sarah the promised child sooner. That is a question for heaven. I do know, however, that I've also been prone to pray about something—and then take matters into my own hands when it does not look like God will come through.

While we are waiting, let's ask God to show us how to pray according to his will. Let's trust in his goodness toward us and all that concerns us . . . even if we have to wait.

Anneliese

PRAY

God, help me discern when to act and when to wait. Give me wisdom to pray according to your will.

SAVOR

When have you been tempted to act rather than wait on God? How can you wait for God today?

Week 13, Day 2
CLOUD OF GOD'S LEADING

By day the Lord went ahead of them in a pillar of cloud to guide them on their way and by night in a pillar of fire to give them light, so that they could travel by day or night. Neither the pillar of cloud by day nor the pillar of fire by night left its place in front of the people. —EXODUS 13:21-22 (NIV)

While visiting my daughter in Saskatchewan one summer, I saw an amazing cloud. My grandsons and I were on the way home from swimming lessons when we saw it. We were simply stunned by the beauty of the sun's rays shining out from around its edges. We commented on how it reminded us of the cloud that God sent to lead the Israelites through the wilderness.

Then recently, I came across a photograph of a different cloud, this one at sunset. It looked as if it were alive with flame. That cloud reminded me of the pillar of fire that led the people of God by night.

These clouds made me wonder what life was like for the Hebrew people. After years of being enslaved to Pharaoh, the Israelites fled Egypt into the wilderness. They had lived all their lives in the cities of Egypt, with its familiar streets and buildings and neighborhoods. They knew nothing else. Now they were in the midst of a featureless desert, without roads or signs to guide them. They must have felt lost and directionless. I imagine they were fearful of the dangers that lurked in those unknown lands, and uncertain as to what the future held.

But they were God's people, and God knew their need for guidance. So he provided direction and comfort for them in the pillar of cloud by day and the pillar of fire by night. Seeing those pillars in front of them must have provided much reassurance to Moses and to all the people.

The magnificent clouds I see these days do not lead me in quite the same specific way that clouds led the Israelites. But clouds can still be reminders to me of God's amazing power to lead and guide us when we are disoriented and alone.

Bev

PRAY

God, thank you for the ways that you have led me to this point. Lead me today, and surround me with your cloud of comfort and direction.

SAVOR

What type of leading do you need today? What type of direction are you seeking from God?

Week 13, Day 3

GOD NEVER LETS GO

The Lord is my light and my salvation; whom shall I fear? The Lord is the stronghold of my life; of whom shall I be afraid? —PSALM 27:1 (ESV)

My husband and I have had many opportunities to introduce our children to the great outdoors. But never did I imagine that as adults they would continue to scale the highest mountain peaks! These days, as I watch them pack their mountain gear, I see ropes and harnesses, ice axes and picks, mountain boots, crampons, and helmets. They are equipping themselves carefully, looking for a safe passage through the rough terrain in order to eventually summit.

Our journey through life was never meant to be easy. As we travel through the rough terrain, we need to continuously check our gear to make sure it's intact. Are we trusting God as our guide and leader? Or have we begun to slide through some of the cracks and crevices, becoming disillusioned with life's twists and turns? What do we do when we face a steep incline and feel we just can't go one more step?

I need to keep a slow, steady pace, putting one foot in front of the other, making every day count. I need to acknowledge God the

Creator and let him be my Guide. I need to take time to listen to his Word and apply the Scriptures to my life.

One of my favorite songs is "You Never Let Go" by Matt Redman. When I walked into church on a recent Sunday morning, our worship leader was singing this song. My heart skipped a beat as I remembered the many times I have listened to that song and worshiped God.

I like to imagine God going with my kids as they climb mountains. On real mountains or the mountains of life, we can sing to our God with confidence, "You never let go!"

We must continue to trudge through life even when the way is difficult. There is a light of hope for all of us, because one day we will eventually summit.

Marg

PRAY
God, thank you for never letting go of me. Help me to never let go of you.

SAVOR
Which promise from God can you claim for your climb today?

Week 13, Day 4
A MOTHER'S INFLUENCE

But let your adorning be the hidden person of the heart with the imperishable beauty of a gentle and quiet spirit, which in God's sight is very precious. —1 PETER 3:4 (ESV)

When I was little, I spent most of my time with my mother. I have been thinking lately about how much she influenced who I have become. I close my eyes and try to remember the way things were in my home: Plastic on the windows to keep out the stiff northeast winds. Floral linoleum. Homemade clothes. Long winter evenings. Knitting lessons.

I remember my mother often being bone-weary, and her hands were always busy with cooking and mending. Still, she always gave me the impression that I was worthwhile. Though she didn't have much time to read, she read the one book that she loved most. She read her Bible, and she listened to her favorite radio Bible programs each weekday morning.

In the best of times and the worst of times, her faith in God remained, and I saw it lived out from my childhood to my own years of mothering young children. I value that she protected me by having boundaries for me before I had enough sense to create my own. She loved my dad well. She always kissed me goodnight.

My mother's life affected me in the ways that matter most. She had the beauty of a gentle and quiet spirit, which were great gifts to me and my family. I pray that I have passed on a portion of her loving and committed spirit to my children and grandchildren.

Lorella

I can do all this through him who gives
me strength. —PHILIPPIANS 4:13 (NIV)

Our family recently celebrated my father-in-law's one hundredth birthday. We call him Papa, and his grandchildren call him Opa. During his birthday celebration, someone asked Opa this question: "What is your favorite motto?"

He answered, "*Gott kann,*" which means "God can."

Two very simple words, short and to the point. But those words became a powerful statement for our family. During the weekend, we listened to stories from young and old. After a niece or a nephew or grandchild would share a story from her or his life, we would all respond by saying Opa's motto: "God can!" As families left at the end of the weekend, we smiled and waved. But we did not say goodbye; rather, we said to each other, "God can!" These words have been etched on our hearts forever.

As authors of *Mennonite Girls Can Cook*, we have formed deep friendships, and we communicate daily with each other and pray for each other online. This has become a huge blessing for all of us. Over the years, we have adopted that same phrase, and many times we sign off our messages to each other by saying "*Gott kann!*"

Times have changed dramatically during the past one hundred years. But I am so encouraged to know that the same faith that my father-in-law has handed down still holds strong for us today. I hope that whatever you are experiencing, wherever you are, you too can echo the same words: "God can!"

PRAY	SAVOR
God, all things are within your power. Help me to believe in you, and give me strength to act in your power.	*How might your outlook change if you declared every day: "God can"?*

Week 13, Day 6
GOOD EYESIGHT

For now we see only a reflection as in a mirror; then we shall see face to face. Now I know in part; then I shall know fully, even as I am fully known. —1 CORINTHIANS 13:12 (NIV)

Light and vision have been recurring subjects of conversation in our house lately. My husband had a cataract removed first from one eye, and then, a month later, the other. I had the procedure done several years ago, and so I understand when he describes the changes this is making in how he sees.

In cataract surgery, the doctor removes the clouded lens from your eye and replaces it with a soft plastic lens. The new lens is usually a corrective one so that your vision is improved.

During the month between having the left eye and right eye done, I remember opening my left eye and closing my right, and then opening my right and closing my left, to see how differently things appeared. From seeing things as indistinct blurs to seeing sharply, from seeing things with a subdued and yellowed cast to seeing bright, clear colors: the difference between the "good" eye and the "bad" was remarkable.

The Bible tells us that the commands of the Lord are radiant, giving light to the eyes. When we obey his commands, God's will is made clear to us, illuminating our daily walk.

As Paul says in 1 Corinthians, our limited and often flawed perceptions here on earth will be clear and vibrant when we see Christ face to face. What we see as negative experiences while we are going through them will be shown as blessings when seen through God's perfect lens.

May we see the world as God does—with vision that is clear, illuminating, and true. And may we look forward to that magnificent day in the future when we will see our Savior face to face!

PRAY

God, lend me your eyes today. Help me to see others with your true and clear vision.

SAVOR

Close your eyes and review the day ahead or the day you just experienced. How would God see it?

Week 13, Day 7

COMMENCEMENT

The twenty-four elders fall down before him who is seated on the throne and worship him who lives forever and ever. They cast their crowns before the throne, saying, "Worthy are you, our Lord and God, to receive glory and honor and power." —REVELATION 4:10-11 (ESV)

I recently had the privilege of attending my granddaughter's high school commencement ceremony. All graduates had their moment on center stage. Their achievements, scholarships, and plans for the future were noted, and each was presented with a diploma and an official photo. In his speech, the valedictorian pointed out that the word *commencement* does not indicate the end of something but rather the beginning.

As I sat, listening and watching, I realized how this event paralleled another graduation facing all of us. One day we will "graduate" from this earthly life, and people will gather to remember our journey. We call the service a funeral, or a memorial service, or a celebration of life. I have never heard a funeral called a commencement—and yet would that not be an appropriate name?

Death is not the end of life but the commencement of a new life—one that is eternal. If we have been born into God's family, and if we have lived our lives in loving relationship with him and in obedience to his Word, then we will have our moment before God. He will acknowledge our earthly journey with his praise!

Hopefully we will we hear the words "Well done, good and faithful servant! You have been faithful with a few things; I will put you in charge of many things. Come and share your master's happiness!" (Matthew 25:23 NIV).

At the end of my granddaughter's graduation, a deafening cheer rose from the graduates as they threw their caps high into the air. I visualize a coming moment when eternity shall commence and multitudes, in white robes, will stand before the throne of God. I imagine that great crowd throwing their crowns at Jesus' feet. What a joyful celebration that will be!

Julie

PRAY

God, prepare my spirit for the true commencement. Thank you for the celebration that I have to look forward to in heaven.

SAVOR

Meditate on the celebration that awaits us in heaven. What can you do today to prepare for that great commencement of eternal life?

Recipe
STRAWBERRY SHEET PIE

Serves 20

Pastry
- 5 cups / 1.25 L flour
- 4 teaspoons / 20 ml brown sugar
- 2 teaspoons / 10 ml salt
- 1 teaspoon / 5 ml baking powder
- 1 pound / 454 g lard, cubed

- 1 egg
- 1 tablespoon / 15 ml white vinegar
- Enough cold water to make 1 cup / 250 ml liquid

1. Measure flour, brown sugar, salt, and baking powder into a large, wide bowl. Stir with a fork to distribute the dry ingredients.
2. Cut lard into the flour with a pastry blender until it forms small crumbs, similar in consistency to oatmeal.
3. Crack egg into a measuring cup and whisk lightly. Add vinegar and fill with water to the 1-cup / 250-ml line.
4. Drizzle the water-egg-vinegar mixture over dry ingredients and stir with a fork until a shaggy dough forms.
5. Turn out onto a floured counter, press together, and shape into a loaf.
6. Divide the pastry into half. Divide one of theses halves into two parts so that you have three pieces altogether.
7. Wrap the two smaller pieces separately in plastic wrap. The two smaller pieces will be enough for one double-crust pie or two pie shells. This extra may be refrigerated for several days, or frozen until needed.
8. Preheat oven to 400° F / 205° C.
9. For this dessert, take the large piece of pastry, place it on floured pastry mat or well-floured counter, and roll it out until it is large enough to come up the sides of a 13 x 18-inch / 33 x 46-cm baking

sheet. Roll the pastry up onto your rolling pin and transfer to the baking sheet. Trim the edges along the top.

10. Prick the dough with a fork every couple of inches and line the pastry with foil, pressing firmly onto the pastry, covering it all.

11. Bake 10 minutes, then remove the foil and bake a few more minutes until evenly browned. Do not underbake: the pastry should be crisp. Cool for 1 hour before adding the cream cheese layer (recipe follows). In the meantime, prepare the strawberry filling.

Strawberry Filling

- ¾ cup / 175 ml sugar
- ⅓ cup / 75 ml cornstarch
- 2 cups / 500 ml cold water
- 1 (3-ounce / 90-g) package strawberry gelatin
- 4 pounds / 1.8 kg strawberries, finely diced (enough to make 6 cups / 1.5 L)

1. Combine sugar and cornstarch in a large pot and stir to blend.
2. Add the water and bring to a boil, stirring the whole time.
3. Add gelatin and stir to dissolve.
4. Stir in diced strawberries. Let the mixture cool until it comes to room temperature. In the meantime, prepare the cream cheese layer.

Cream Cheese Layer

- 1 pound / 500 g light or regular cream cheese, softened
- ½ cup / 125 ml white sugar
- 2 tablespoons / 30 ml instant vanilla pudding
- ½ cup / 125 ml heavy whipping cream
- Juice of half a lemon

1. Beat softened cream cheese with the remaining ingredients. Carefully spread evenly over cooled pastry crust. Chill while the strawberry filling is cooling.
2. Spoon cooled strawberry filling onto chilled cream cheese layer. Chill in the refrigerator.

Whipped Cream Topping

- 2 cups / 500 ml whipping cream
- ½ cup / 125 ml sugar
- 2 (0.35-ounce / 10-g) packages whipping cream stabilizer, or 2 tablespoons / 30 ml instant vanilla pudding

1. Beat cream, sugar, and whipping cream stabilizer or instant pudding until stiff peaks form.
2. Remove layered pie from refrigerator. Using a pastry bag with a large star tip, pipe mounds of whipped cream topping on top of the strawberry layer. There should be enough topping to portion the pie into 20 sections.
3. Refrigerate until serving.

There was a time when fresh strawberries were eaten only for several weeks each year. While the local ones are the best, strawberries are available almost year-round on grocery shelves. Make the pastry a day ahead to save time, but serve the finished sheet pie the same day you make it for best texture and flavor. This sheet pie makes 20 generous servings but can be easily stretched to serve up to 25 people.

Lovella

THE AUTHORS

 LOVELLA SCHELLENBERG enjoys farm life together with her husband, Terry, near the west coast of British Columbia. Having been married thirty-eight years, they are enjoying this season of their life with both sons married and the blessing of daughters-in-law and five delightful grands. They love camping near the beautiful coastal beaches and in the mountains. Picking ripe produce from her vegetable garden, taking in the fragrance of fresh roses, and watching storm clouds remind her that she is surrounded by God's beautiful creations and blessings. Lovella and Terry are members of Northview Community Church in Abbotsford, where they mentor couples preparing for marriage.

ANNELIESE FRIESEN and her husband, Herb, have made their home in the beautiful Fraser Valley of British Columbia, where they have raised three children. They are the proud grandparents of ten sweet grandchildren. Together they have been involved in various ministries  related to care and hospitality for nearly thirty-five years. She is now in what she calls the fall season of her life, enjoying the vibrant colors of the changes this season has brought with it. Her desire is to encourage younger women in their roles as wives and mothers, being grateful to her Lord and Savior for his wonderful provision for such a time as this.

 JUDY WIEBE and her husband, Elmer, live in the Fraser Valley of British Columbia, where they are involved in the family dairy farm operation. Their three grown children, their spouses, and seven delightful grands all live nearby. Judy enjoys spending time in the great outdoors, creating things in her kitchen or sewing room, and traveling whenever possible, but her favorite times are those spent with friends and family. She attends Central Community Church in Chilliwack.

BETTY REIMER lives in Steinbach, Manitoba, with her husband, John. She and her husband owned and operated a farm and garden equipment business for twenty-eight years and are now retired. They are blessed with two daughters, one son, one son-in-law, and four grandchildren. Betty attends Evangelical Fellowship Church. She loves spending time with her family and friends and enjoys baking, reading, gardening, and traveling.

 BEV KLASSEN works with her husband, Harv, in a home-based business in Rosedale, British Columbia. They have three married children and seven grandchildren, who daily bless their lives. Bev enjoys cooking and entertaining, and she and Harv often host family and friends in their home. Bev's favorite activities are taking pictures, reading, gardening, and making cards. She and Harv do a lot of traveling for business and pleasure, taking road trips by car or motorcycle, along with occasional trips overseas. Greendale Mennonite Brethren Church has been her church home for forty-five years.

CHARLOTTE PENNER lives in Winnipeg, Manitoba, with her husband, Tony. She is a mom of two daughters, one son, and two sons-in-law. Charlotte and her husband attend Douglas Mennonite Church and are involved in a variety of ways. She enjoys being with family and friends, attending Bible study, ministering to those who are hurting, and providing spontaneous hospitality. She likes to cook and bake, and there is always room for more around her table.

ELLEN BAYLES lives in the Seattle area with her husband, Greg. She was born and raised in southern California and earned a bachelor of arts degree in home economics with elementary teaching credentials. She was an elementary school teacher until her first child was born. Ellen and Greg raised two sons and a daughter. All three of their children are married and live in different areas of Washington State. Ellen enjoys homemaking, traveling, and photography. Her husband is a pharmacist. She and Greg are members of Northshore Community Church in Kirkland, Washington.

JULIE KLASSEN was born and raised in the Fraser Valley of British Columbia, where she married, lived, and worked—never far from a sewing machine—until health challenges demanded life changes. Ten years ago, Julie and Vic, her husband of fifty years, moved to Chilliwack and are now both enjoying retirement. They live within walking distance of their daughter, son-in-law, and two beautiful granddaughters. Julie enjoys spending time with family and friends as well as reading, writing, baking, sewing, and she is also involved in their home church, Chilliwack Alliance.

 KATHY MCLELLAN grew up on Vancouver Island, British Columbia, where she met her husband, Scot. They have been married for thirty-eight years and have two married daughters and five precious grandchildren. Kathy and Scot can be found camping in some of British Columbia's most beautiful spots. Their joy in serving is through random acts of kindness in unexpected places. They attend Main Street Church in Chilliwack.

MARG BARTEL was born and raised in the Fraser Valley of British Columbia. She met her husband, John, at a farm sale, and together they continued a farming career. Later in life, when farming no longer demanded her strong support, Marg completed her baccalaureate degree, thus giving her new opportunities to work outside the home. Marg is a sports enthusiast and enjoys traveling. She also enjoys the opportunity to be actively involved in the life of her family, friends, community, and church.

COOK ALONG WITH THE MENNONITE GIRLS

Mennonite Girls Can Cook
Hardcover. 208 pages. $24.99 USD. 9780836195538

Mennonites are known for their wholesome cooking, and *Mennonite Girls Can Cook* will not disappoint. From heritage dishes to comfort foods, the more than one hundred enticing, easy-to-prepare recipes are bound to become trusted favorites.

MENNONITE GIRLS CAN COOK
Traditions of Food and Faith

BUY THEIR BESTSELLING COOKBOOKS

Mennonite Girls Can Cook Celebrations
Hardcover. 320 pages. $29.99 USD. 9780836196757

From succulent soufflé to mouthwatering muffins, the Mennonite Girls share recipes to honor all of life. Filled with devotional reflections, personal stories, and beautiful photos, this book will become your guide for life's celebrations.